Advanced
Scrollsaw Proje

Advanced Scrollsaw Projects

GUILD OF MASTER CRAFTSMAN PUBLICATIONS LTD

This collection first published 2001 by
Guild of Master Craftsman Publications Ltd,
Castle Place, 166 High Street, Lewes,
East Sussex BN7 1XU

© GMC Publications 2001

ISBN 1 86108 191 X

A catalogue record of this book is available from the British Library

Front cover photographs: (clockwise) Terry Lawrence, Bob Curran,
Jack Hudson, Ivor Carlyle

Back cover photographs: (from top to bottom) Christine Richardson,
Ralph Sinnot, Ivor Carlyle, Christine Richardson, John Burke

Article photography:
Anthony Bailey (p. 53), Ivor Carlyle (pp.13 (bottom),14–16, 46–49,
53 (bottom), 54–56), John Everett (pp. 9–12, 19–22),
Jack Hudson (pp. 89–94), Terry Lawrence (pp. 34–37, 68–71,
83–86, 103–106), Jennie Loader (pp. 113–115),
Christine Richardson (pp. 13 (top), 24–27, 29–31, 97–101),
Ralph Sinnott (pp. 62–64)

Printed and bound by Kyodo Printing (Singapore) under the
supervision of MRM Graphics, Winslow, Buckinghamshire, UK

Contents

Note and Measurements   vi

Introduction   1

Part One Intermediate Projects

Folding bowl   3
This little space-saving container, designed by
Bob Curran, is ideal for fruit or even bread rolls

Plain or pearl?   9
John Everett explains the mini-gingerbread
technique

Bounding bunnies   13
As an alternative to chocolate eggs and bunnies
Ivor Carlyle creates something a little different
for Easter

Time to reflect   19
John Everett creates a stunning mirror clock
that features skills in intricate cutting

Tied up in Celtic knotwork   24
Celtic designs are ideal for jewellery as John
Burke explains

Let there be light   29
Traditional 18th-century Swedish style is given
a contemporary colour treatment by
Christine Richardson

Jigsaurus acrylicus   34
Little devotees of dinosaurs and whales will be
delighted with these jigsaws, cut by Terry
Lawrence from Altuglas acrylic sheet

How time flies   46
Ivor Carlyle brings you Britain's favourite bird
as a wall plaque or clock

Part Two Advanced Projects

All aboard   53
This beautifully crafted engine design is sure to
be popular with train enthusiasts whatever their
age. Project and photography by Ivor Carlyle

The time, date and place   62
Ralph Sinnott goes back to his childhood with
this fascinating project

Vasilissa and the White Horseman   68
Based on an illustration by Russian artist
Ivan Bilibin, Terry Lawrence creates a three-
dimensional picture

Riding with the Red Horseman   74
Terry Lawrence introduces the second of three
horsemen interpretations

Black Horseman   83
Terry Lawrence presents the third and final
multi-layered, three-dimensional picture in the set

Luxury dining   89
Jack Hudson puts the scrollsaw to work on this
practical and easy-to-make set of table, chairs
and bench for toddlers

Hall of mirrors   97
Sweeping lines in the Art Nouveau style make
this hall mirror and coat rack by Christine
Richardson a perfect partner for the period home

A moment of history   103
Terry Lawrence gives a brief history lesson with
his interpretation of the Bayeux tapestry

Advanced cutting   113
In this final section, Jeff Loader deals with
the techniques required for advanced
cutting operations

Metric and imperial conversion charts   117

Index   118

Note

Every effort has been made to ensure that the information in this book is accurate at the time of writing but inevitably prices, specifications, and availability of tools will change from time to time. Readers are therefore urged to contact manufacturers or suppliers for up-to-date information before ordering tools.

Measurements

Throughout the book instances may be found where a metric measurement has fractionally varying imperial equivalents, usually within $\frac{1}{16}$in either way. This is because in each particular case the closest imperial equivalent has been given. A mixture of metric and imperial measurements should never be used – always use either one or the other.

See also detailed metric/imperial conversion charts on page 117.

Introduction

Scrollsawing is one of the fastest growing crafts of modern times. Some of the world's best known exponents of the art reveal their secrets to lead the way forward with new techniques and developments.

All the authors are acknowledged in the world of the scrollsaw for their imagination and expertise, and many are professional craftsmen. The reader, therefore, can be confident that the projects featured throughout are uncluttered by unproven practices and theories, outdated techniques or impractical approaches. All represent a valid source of up-to-the-minute information.

In these pages you will find fresh project ideas, using the wide variety of materials that can be worked with the scrollsaw. An easy to follow step-by-step format ensures success, whatever the skill level of the reader.

Ideas and inspirations from the world of the scrollsaw give the reader the capability to produce unlimited and very beautiful works without the assistance of other machining processes.

Paul Richardson
Managing Editor (Magazines)

Part One
Intermediate Projects

Folding bowl

This little space-saving container, designed by **Bob Curran**, is ideal for fruit or even bread rolls

The folding bowl in this project is highly flexible in its potential uses. It also looks nice full of pot pourri or used to display flowers. It features one major advantage, as it can be pushed flat for storage when not in use.

Although the piece was relatively small when completed, as a scrollsaw project it was a major challenge. Could I cut and stay on a line that was continuously curving and was in total, nearly 3m (9ft) long. I must admit it was a bit of an effort, but the result was quite pleasing.

Materials, tools

- Main body   1 off   250mm x 22mm x 260mm
- Foot   1 off   20mm x 35mm x 242mm
- Screw brass 2 off   No 8 Round head x 25mm
- Screw brass 3 off   No 8 CSK head x 30mm
- PVA glue

- Hegner scrollsaw
- Blade, reverse-tooth type
- Orbital sander
- Drill
- Drill bits 2mm & 4mm dia
- Aluminium oxide paper,
  grade 220
- Pencil compass
- Sash clamps
- Cauls
- G-clamp

Ensuring timber is knot-free

It was essential that the piece of timber I used for the main body had no knots or other faults in it. Any such blemishes might have caused a breakage when the unit was pushed into shape.

I used pine, but a hardwood such as ash would have looked nice. As I did not have any timber that was wide enough and was blemish-free, I glued together a number of strips to give me the width I needed. These were of course of the required standard. Bar clamps, cauls and G-clamps were used to ensure all the strips were kept level with each other while the glue dried. After gluing up the wood, the assembly was sanded on both sides with an orbital sander.

Marking out

1 Before marking out the outer shape and other details, which are shown in the pattern section, I attached a small piece of thin plywood to the centre of the blank with a piece of double-sided adhesive tape. This protected the surface from the dual compass point positions needed in the marking out. The outside shape was drawn first, then the inner disc.

2 The procedure for marking out the quasi-spiral line cut from position 'A', was to draw a semicircle 50mm (2in) radius from the main centre point. Next, another centre point was marked on the horizontal centre line 3.5mm (⅛in) to the left of the main centre point. The compass point was then put at this new centre point and the compass pencil lined up with the end of the previously drawn semicircle.

3 Another semicircle was then drawn. The compass point was then returned to the main centre point. The compass pencil was then lined up with the end of the second semicircle and the third semicircle drawn. This procedure, of draw semicircle, move compass point, move compass pencil, draw semicircle was repeated until position 'C' was reached.

4 Having set the 50mm (2in) radius and the second centre point 3.5mm (1.8in) to the left, no further measuring was required. The radii detailed on Fig 2 just confirms this procedure.

Scrollsawing can now begin

The blade I used was the reverse-tooth type. I ensured that several of the opposed teeth were above the table top before the cut was commenced. For all the cuts I let the blade and timber thickness dictate the speed of feed.

The first cut was the outside shape. The second cut was the circular inner disc. This was started from a 2mm (⁵⁄₆₄in) diameter hole which was just large enough to pass the blade through, drilled at position 'B'.

The small indent left in the outer frame was later filled with filler.

For the final cut, which was the 'BIG' one, the saw table was tilted to an angle of 3°, the lower side being to the left. Again the cut was started from a 2mm (⁵⁄₆₄in) diameter hole, drilled at position 'A'. The

cut was made in one continuous operation, terminating at position 'C'. Fortunately the phone didn't ring during this operation. The disc was then opened up and all the newly cut corners were lightly sanded.

Foot

The foot was tackled next, see Patterns. When I had completed cutting the first radius I was at a loss why the end was not square. I knew I was cutting wood 35mm (1⅜in) thick but the amount of 'out of squareness', was ridiculous. This was because I had forgotten to reset the table back to the horizontal position.

After a final sanding all over, the bowl and feet were ready for assembly. Three 2mm (⁵⁄₆₄in) diameter pilot holes were drilled in the bottom of the outer frame. The centre foot was then screwed in position, just tight enough to allow it to swivel. The two outer feet were glued and screwed on. The gap between the inner and outer feet was to enable the centre foot to swivel. The two 4mm (⁵⁄₃₂in) diameter holes for the swivel screws were then drilled in the outer frame and the circular centre piece was placed in position.

Four pieces of thin card were pushed in between them to hold the inner disc concentric with the outer frame. Using a

small awl the positions of the holes were marked on the edge of the inner disc. Pilot holes, 2mm (⁵⁄₆₄in) diameter were then drilled in the disc. Care was taken to ensure they didn't go right through top of the bowl. These pilot holes were to make sure there was no splitting when the screws were put in.

The two round head screws were tightened just enough to hold the bowl level when it was opened out. The opening out was done gently and care was taken to ensure the stepped configuration was kept even down the depth of the bowl.

After a good going over with fine abrasive paper the assembly was dusted down. Because the bowl could be used to hold food it was given three coats of vegetable oil. The oil was generously applied with a brush while the bowl was opened out in the reverse direction. In this position as the bottom of the bowl hung down there were gaps between each of the rings. This enabled the rings to be coated all over. This would not have been possible with the bowl opened out in the normal way. When the oil was dry the assembly was given a buff up with a soft cloth and was then ready for use.

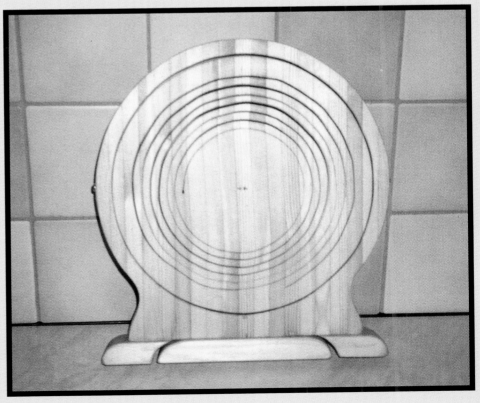

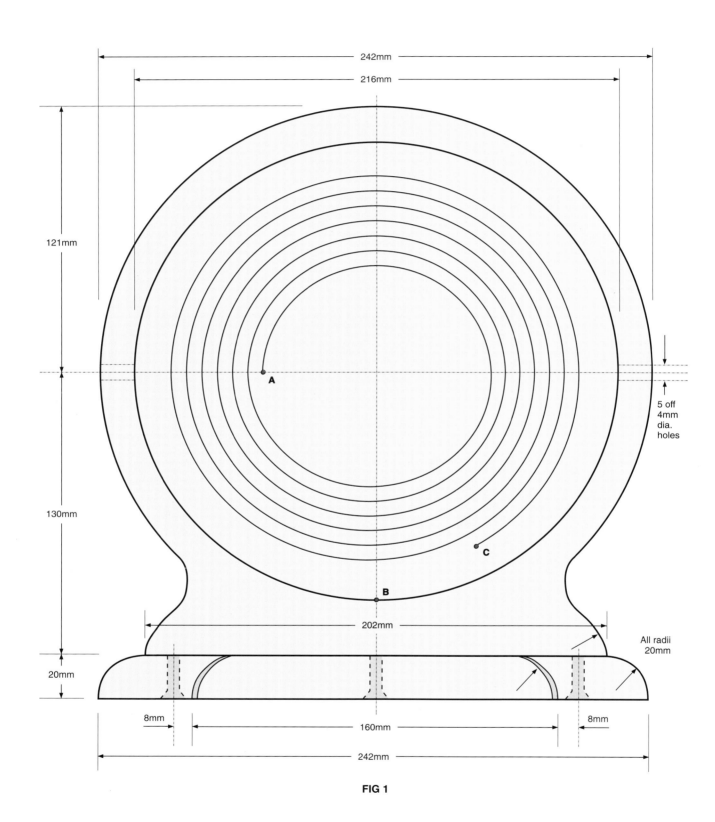

FIG 1

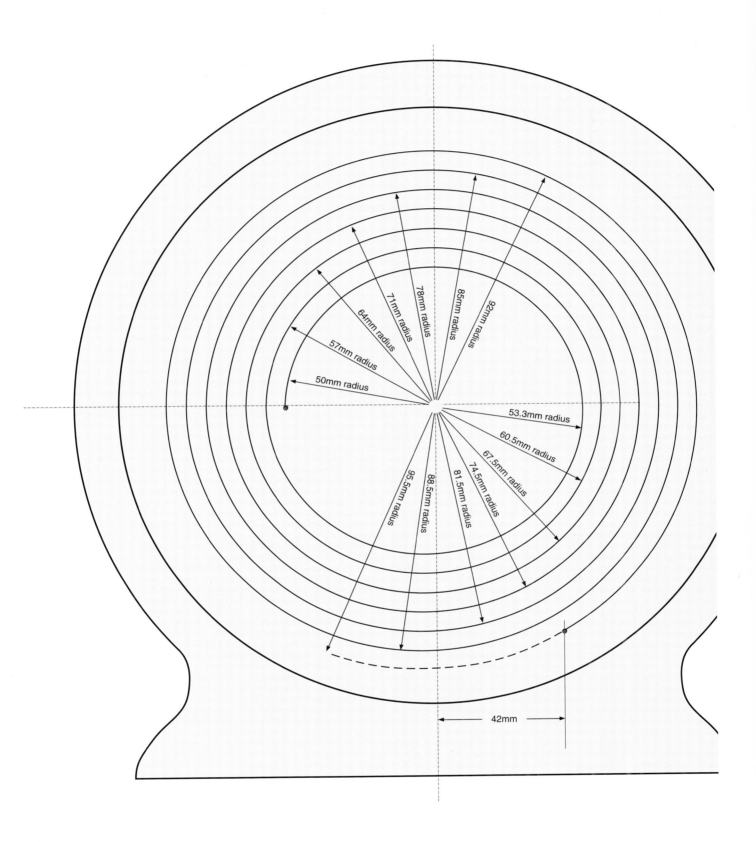

FIG 2

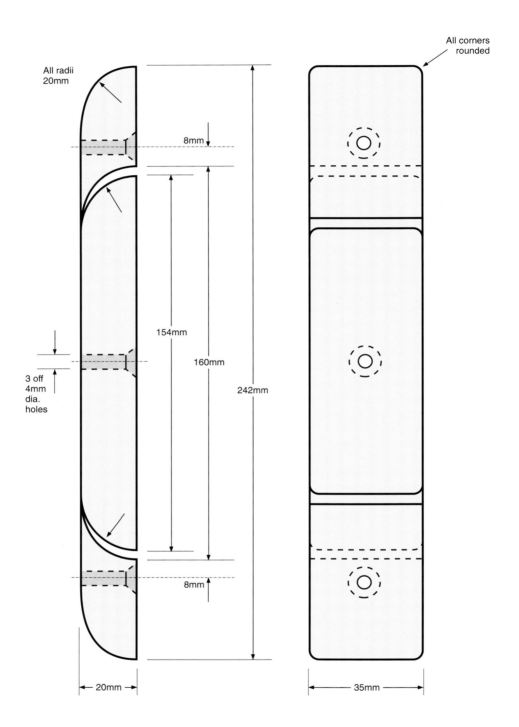

All radii
20mm

All corners
rounded

8mm

154mm

160mm

242mm

3 off
4mm
dia.
holes

8mm

20mm

35mm

FIG 3

Plain or pearl?

John Everett
explains the mini-gingerbread technique

There are times when it is not practical to make ornate joints in wood, due perhaps to time constraints or the sheer number required. It could also be that the cost of the additional time involved cannot be justified. This was the case in point that gave rise to this particular application of the Victorian gingerbread technique. This involves making up small decorative pieces which are usually employed to adorn otherwise plain items of furniture and the like. In this instance, a number of drawers were required for an embroidery cabinet which was rehashed from an older piece of existing cabinet cut down for the purpose.

As the drawers were all slightly different in size, setting up machinery was not practical, even if it had been available. The answer, in view of the need to finish the item quickly, was to simply glue and pin the drawers together. This, of course, left the pins showing at each end of all the drawers which is not really acceptable in any sort of cabinet. However, by designing small pieces of gingerbread as

"It is not difficult to adapt this design to suit your own needs"

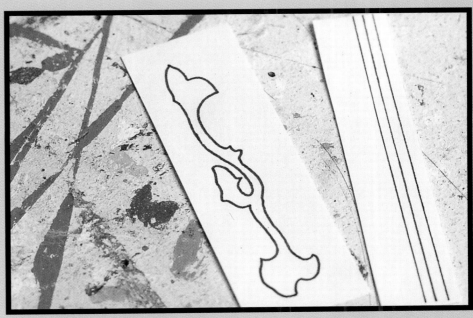

▲ **The pair of cutting patterns ready to mount on the scrap of wood from which the four mini gingerbreads will be cut**

decoration for each end of the drawers, the finished result is attractive and the panel pins are rendered invisible. A classic example of 'if you can't hide it, make a feature out of it'.

The actual pieces of gingerbread were made from a small offcut of the wood left over from the case of the cabinet and so matched the finished item well. The gingerbread shown here requires compound sawing of the finished items, but this is not difficult providing you follow the sequence and take a little care as you work due to the delicate nature of the completed gingerbread. The finished gingerbread is little thicker than a veneer and so needs very careful handling until it has been glued in place. It is not difficult to adapt this design to suit your own needs – you can shorten or extend the connecting stems to suit the nail spacing and enlarge or reduce the leaves according to your own requirements.

1 Begin by making up your cutting pattern. The shape given here is designed so that the

'leaves' cover the areas of the panel pins on the drawers mentioned. The design can be easily modified to allow for alternative nail positioning to be covered by simply making the interconnecting 'stems' either longer or shorter to suit your own particular requirements. The remaining pattern is basically a series of parallel lines, and is used as a guide when slicing the gingerbread into sufficiently thin sections to produce the pattern, without excess thickness. Although this pattern is not strictly essential, it does make life much easier for you than trying to estimate a straight line as you cut out. You do, after all, need the line to be as straight as possible so that the back of the gingerbread will lay flat on the work surface that you want to add it to.

2 Once you have your patterns, cut out a piece of wood slightly larger than your pattern. This is to make sure the longer edges are straight so that you will have a smooth surface when it comes to slicing up the gingerbread. It also makes for easier and more accurate sawing. That done, stick your

Materials, tools

To make this type of gingerbread, you will need:

- Small offcuts of appropriate wood, either a contrast or compliment to whatever you need to apply it to. Do use hardwood as softwood will tend to 'feather' on its cut edge and will never have sufficient strength in any case due to the open grain structure of the timber.

- A fine fretsaw blade of around No 3 gauge or less to make the detail cuts.

- A thicker blade such as a No 7 (a reverse-tooth blade was used here to avoid saw tear-out on the back of the cut pieces) to cut the slices of gingerbread from the block.

- A paper pattern of both the design and the slicing cuts (see text)

- A little Spraymount adhesive and some wood glue or epoxy resin for attaching the finished gingerbread to the cabinet or wherever you intend using it.

◀ Offering up the cutting pattern for the ivy leaf decoration to make sure it can be positioned to hide the panel pins

Sticking the cutting patterns down with a little Spraymount adhesive ▼

cutting patterns in place using a little Spraymount adhesive. Be careful not to apply too much as the finished item will be very delicate and too much scraping to remove the remains of the cutting pattern will damage the gingerbread.

3 Now set up your saw with the fine blade to cut out the main pattern. The piece of wood will be rather small so you will need to take extra care in manoeuvring the work piece as you cut around the outline of the pattern. In all probability, your hold-down device will not be of much use to you owing to the small size of the piece of work so take care where you place your fingers.

4 Begin at one end of the cutting pattern and carefully cut all the way around the pattern so that you end the cut where you started. Do not remove any of the surrounding excess wood as you will need this in order to make the compound cut which will give you the finished 'slices' of gingerbread.

5 Change the blade in your saw to the coarser one. A reverse-tooth blade will be best if you have one, otherwise leave the pattern with its 'waste' in place. Gently sand the back of each slice after you have cut it free from the block of wood. Cut along the straight line making sure you keep it as straight as possible. When you

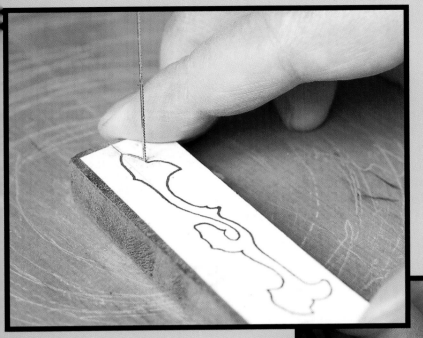

◄ Beginning the cut on the ivy leaf pattern. Begin at one end and continue round the cut with no interruptions so that once the cut has been completed, there will be the ivy leaf pattern and the 'waste' each in one piece. This is important so that they can be reassembled to make the compound cut that will provide the slices from the main piece of gingerbread

The ivy leaf cutout completed. Note that the waste is in one piece with no breaks ▼

The offcut remade into one piece with a couple of strips of adhesive tape so that the slices can be cut off from the main piece ▼

The ivy leaf pattern slices coming away from the main block of wood. Leave the actual ivy leaf decoration in place within the waste wood until the very last moment that you instal it in its final position as it will be very fragile and will not take any physical pressure. Once it has been glued in place and the glue has set thoroughly, there will be no more worries about breakages as it will have become part of the main piece. At this point, it can be brushed with wax, varnish or what you will by way of final decoration ▼

approach the end of the cut, use a 'push stick', which is just a scrap of wood, to apply a little pressure into the final few millimetres of each cut. This will help you avoid slicing a finger. Keep the other hand on the back of the work to steady it through the final part of each cut, making sure the pattern does not move in relation to the waste wood – or you will lose the flatness of the finished slice. If you are not too sure if you can keep things steady enough, apply a strip of adhesive tape along each side of the pattern while you cut the slices.

▲ Using a push stick to make the final part of the slicing cuts to avoid the slice extending to one's fingers!

6 Once you have cut all the slices you need – four were made from the piece shown here which is enough for two drawers – very carefully remove any remains of your cutting patterns from the gingerbread pieces. All that remains now is to check each piece for any gentle sanding that might be required and to stick the gingerbread into place where it is needed.

"If you can't hide it, make a feature out of it"

The finished items ready for installation ▼

A piece of gingerbread in place on the drawer front. Note that it covers the panel pins perfectly ▼

By using the same gingerbread pattern on the fronts of all three drawers of this cabinet, the gingerbread becomes part of the cabinet and appears to be there by design ▼

Bounding bunnies

As an alternative to chocolate eggs and bunnies **Ivor Carlyle** creates something a little different for children this Easter

A wooden bunny with a basket of goodies hung up and displayed as a decoration was my original idea and this could in fact be an option. However, as it neared completion, I decided it would be fun to make him wave at children through the window. To achieve this was quite simple – by stringing up the bunny as a marionette. A matching Easter Bunny egg cup has been made to complement the marionette and can be used to hold a real or chocolate egg.

Construction

All gluing is with PVA woodworking adhesive unless otherwise stated. Tongue-and-groove 7.5mm (⁵⁄₁₆in) pine wood cladding sheets are very cheap and sold in bargain packs in DIY stores. I glued these sheets together to make up the various thicknesses required. Because of the lamination, the soft pine wood is made more stable and less prone to warping and splitting.

1 To make the thickness required, spread the glue evenly on to the TGV pine wood sheets with a piece of scrap ply, and clamp together firmly in a workmate between scrap blocks of thick plywood or blockboard.

Marionette

2 Mark up the body (see Patterns) on to a 15mm (⅝in) thick piece of wood and cut out the inner circular area (I used a No 2 blade) that forms the chest only at a 5° angle. Round off the edge of the disc and the edge of the hole where it faces out.

3 Glue the piece of wood with the hole in it on to a similar size of 30mm (1³⁄₁₆in) thick wood. Mark up the positions of the holes for the neck, arms and legs and drill.

4 Cut out the body with a heavier blade; I used a No 9 double-spaced tooth blade for this job. Note the 5° angle of cut. Round off the edges of the body as shown on the side view in Fig 1 with glass paper or for a quicker result, with a sanding drum on a mini-drill.

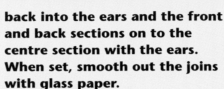

5 Mark up the head section with ears. Drill 1mm (½in) holes in the ears for the scrollsaw blade to be inserted so that the inner ear sections can be fretted out using a No 2 blade. Cut around the exterior with a No 7 blade. Drill the 6mm (¼in) hole for the neck joint.

6 Mark up the front and rear head sections (see Patterns) and drill holes for nose and eyes in the front section before cutting out shapes with a No 7 blade.

7 Trim the inner ear sections so they taper at their base as shown by the dotted line on the side view in Fig 2. Round off the head areas on the front and back head sections and taper off the cheeks. Smooth off with glass paper.

8 Shape the ears with a sharp craft knife and glue the inner ear sections

back into the ears and the front and back sections on to the centre section with the ears. When set, smooth out the joins with glass paper.

9 Mark up the feet and counterbore the 6mm (¼in) holes before cutting out. Cut out the toes and round off their top edge before gluing onto the tops of the feet. Cut out the tail and round off the outer facing edge but do not glue on to the body just yet.

10 Mark up the hands and cuffs and drill the 6mm (¼in) holes before cutting them out. Note there is a 3mm (⅛in) hole in the right hand for the cord on the basket. You can leave the hands flat but it is reasonably easy to whittle with a sharp craft knife the thumb and fingers to shape. Rub them smooth with glass paper and round off the edges of the cuffs before gluing them to the hands.

11 Cut a basket from the cell sections of a papier-mâché egg carton and glue it into the plywood basket rim. Trim flush along the top when set.

12 Use a slower speed for more control while cutting with a No 2 blade.

13 After cutting out the tie, round off its edges.

14 Round off the ends of pieces of dowel as shown in Fig 3 and cut to length on a jig to make the nose and eyes.

15 Cut out the cross-tree parts and drill the holes for the cords, and then glue them together.

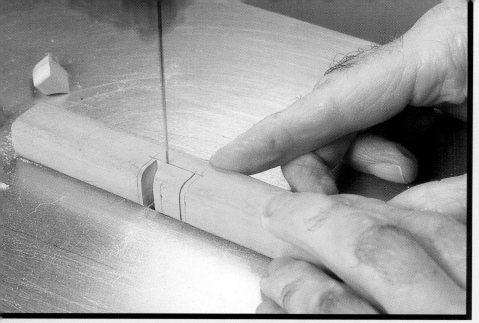

finish, use a non-toxic primer such as Japlac and for the colours Humbrol enamels also certified non-toxic.

Egg Cup

16 Mark up the bunny's egg cup head onto a piece of 7.5mm (⁵⁄₁₆in) wood and drill out the holes for the nose and eyes. Join it to another piece of 7.5mm (⁵⁄₁₆in) wood with double-sided tape and cut around the exterior line only. I used a No 2 blade. Separate the two pieces and cut the top layer into its separate pieces.

17 As with the marionette, round off the ends of pieces of dowel and cut to length on a jig to make the nose and eyes. Cut out the teeth from 1.5mm (¹⁄₁₆in) plywood with a No 2 blade.

18 Mark up the two top egg cup sections and fret out the hole in one at 90° and in the other at 25° to produce an internal bevel. Cut the bottom section out at 45° along three sides and the fourth at 90° as shown in the side view section in Fig 5. Rub the inside of the holes smooth with glass paper before gluing all three sections together. When set, rub the cup section smooth and round off the top edges except those facing the bunny's head.

Taper the inner ear sections as shown on Fig 5 and round off the edges of the head and ears on its top surface. Glue the bottom layer of the head on to the cup.

Finishing

19 I decided to make the finish highlight the wood grain and texture. To achieve this paint the various parts with acrylic colour mixed with acrylic varnish at a ratio of about 1:1. The black for the eyes and pink for the noses can be paint only. If, however, you wish to use a harder gloss enamel

20 Gently rub over with 120 grade glass paper the raised knap areas in particular.

21 Glue the chest disc into the body of the marionette and glue the head and ear sections onto the bottom layer of the head for the egg cup.

22 Give the parts two to three top coats of satin acrylic varnish, smoothing out any coarse areas between coats with glass paper.

Cutting List

Marionette

- 30mm (1³⁄₁₆in) pine
- 1 x body section 82mm (3¼in) diameter
- 15mm (1⁵⁄₂in) pine
- 1 x body front section 82mm (3¼in) diameter
- 1 x chest section 50mm (1¹⁵⁄₁₆in) diameter
- 1 x head and ears section 110mm (4³⁄₈in) x 78mm (21⁄₁₆in)
- 1 x front head section 50mm (2in) x 78mm (2¹¹⁄₁₆in)
- 1 x rear head section 50mm (2in) x 78mm (21⁄₁₆in)
- 1 x tail 32mm (1¼in) diameter
- 2 x feet 65mm (2⁹⁄₁₆in) x 38mm (1½in)

- 2 x hands 43mm (1¹¹⁄₁₆in) x 39mm (1½in)
- 2 x cuffs 36mm (1³⁄₈in) x 25mm (1in)
- 7.5mm (⁵⁄₁₆in) pine
- 2 x toes 38mm (1½in) diameter
- 1 x tie 49mm (1¹⁵⁄₁₆in) x 13mm (½in)
- 6mm (¼in) plywood
- 1 x basket rim 62mm (2⁷⁄₁₆in) x 80mm (3¹⁄₈in)
- 1.5 (¹⁄₁₆in) plywood
- 1 x teeth 14mm (⁹⁄₁₆in) x 10mm (³⁄₈in)
- 12mm (½in) dowel
- 1 x nose 21mm (1³⁄₁₆in)
- 6mm (¼in) dowel
- 2 x eyes 16mm (⁵⁄₈in)
- 1 x neck 48mm (1¹⁵⁄₁₆in)
- 15mm (⁹⁄₁₆in) x 19mm (¾in) beech
- 2 x crosstree parts 130mm (5¹⁄₈in)

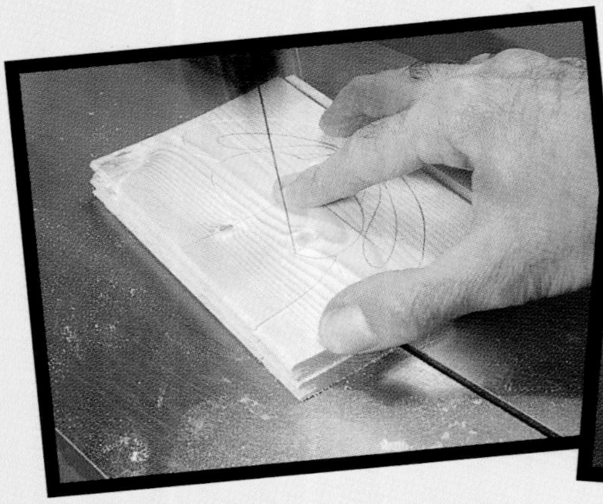

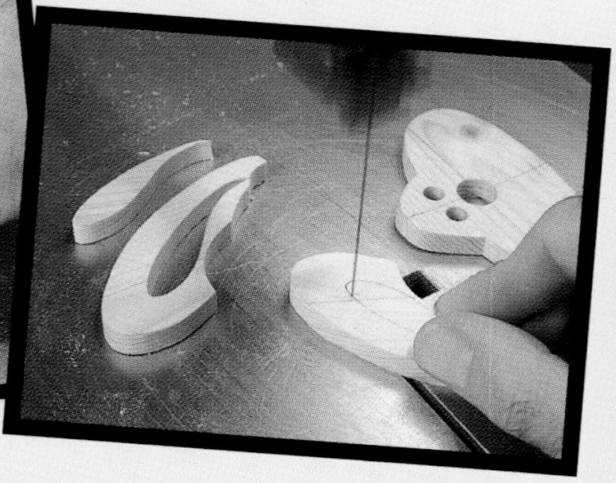

Bunny Egg Cup

- 7.5mm (5/16in) pine
- 1 x head top section 136mm (5 3/8in) x 57mm (2 1/4in)
- 1 x head bottom section 136mm (5 3/8in) x 57mm (2 1/4in)
- 3 x cup sections 60mm (2 3/8in) x 60mm (2 3/8in)
- 1.5mm (1/16in) plywood
- 1 x teeth 14mm (9/16in) x 10mm (3/8in)
- 12mm (1/2in) dowel
- 1 x nose 14mm (9/16in)
- 6mm (1/4in) dowel
- 2 x eyes 11mm (7/16in)

23 **Carefully drill 1.5mm (1/16in) holes through the marionette's hands, feet and between the ears. The reason for drilling these after painting is that they so easily fill up.**

24 **Glue on to the egg cup and marionette the noses, eyes and teeth. Also glue the tie on to the marionette's body and then attach its head with the dowel neck joint to the body.**

25 **To make the arms and legs for the marionette, wrap pieces of gumstrip (do not use self-adhesive tape) around the crepe cord to prevent it unravelling. This allows spaces between the tape of 40mm (1 9/16in) for the arms and 65mm (2 9/16in) for the legs. Cut the pieces of cord to length with a sharp knife. Fix the ends of the cords covered with tape into the arm and leg holes of the body and into the holes of the hands and feet with epoxy resin.**

26 **Tie a thread on to the marionette's head by passing it through the hole between the ears and tie a loop. Tie the other end to the hole in the crosstree opposite the screw eye. Note: the screw eye should face towards the marionette. The length is optional. I made mine so the distance between the cross-tree and the feet is 540mm (21in). To assist with the threading, clamp the crosstree to the corner of a table or desk to suspend the marionette. Pass the ends of two threads through the top of each toe and make a thick knot underneath. Put some glue on the knot and pull up into the holes and allow to set before attaching to the remaining holes in the crosstree. Tie a thread onto one of the hands, making a loop. Pass the other end of the thread through the screw eye on the crosstree and tie onto the other hand so that the hands are level at about waist height on the bunny.**

27 **Knot the end of a piece of 2mm (1/16in) cord and pass it through from underneath one of the holes in the basket. Place the cord through the hole in the bunny's right hand and through the other hole in the basket and secure with a knot. Put some glue on the cord where it passes through the hand to prevent it slipping.**

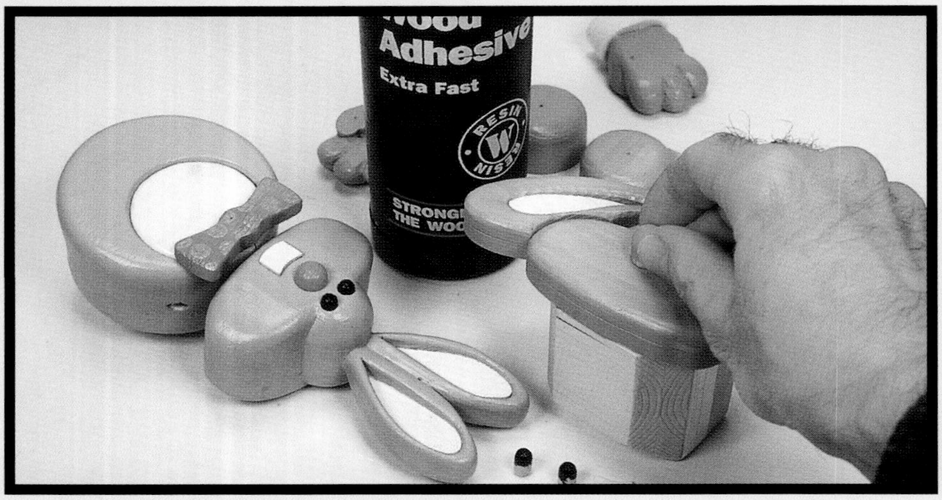

Finishing

- Acrylic paints (Humbrol or other non-toxic equivalents). Colours suggested, blue, white, pink, black, orange and silver.
- Acrylic Satin Varnish (Rustins which is certified as non-toxic).

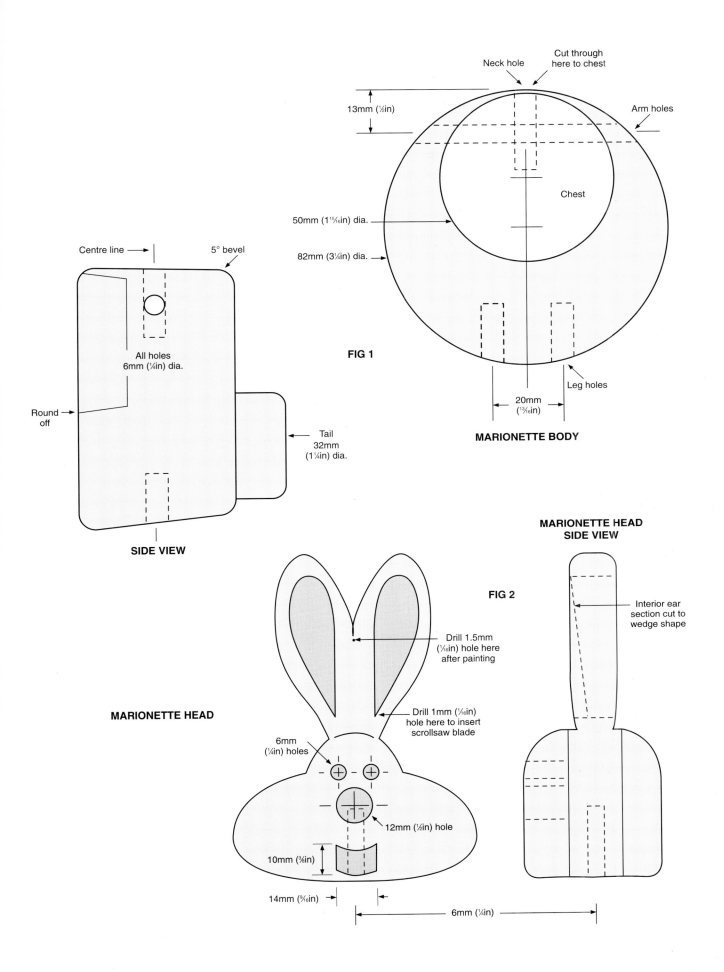

Neck hole

Cut through here to chest

Arm holes

13mm (½in)

Chest

50mm (1⁵⁄₁₆in) dia.

82mm (3¼in) dia.

Leg holes

20mm (¹³⁄₁₆in)

FIG 1

MARIONETTE BODY

Centre line

5° bevel

All holes 6mm (¼in) dia.

Round off

Tail 32mm (1¼in) dia.

SIDE VIEW

MARIONETTE HEAD SIDE VIEW

FIG 2

Drill 1.5mm (¹⁄₁₆in) hole here after painting

Interior ear section cut to wedge shape

Drill 1mm (¹⁄₁₆in) hole here to insert scrollsaw blade

MARIONETTE HEAD

6mm (¼in) holes

12mm (½in) hole

10mm (³⁄₈in)

14mm (⁹⁄₁₆in)

6mm (¼in)

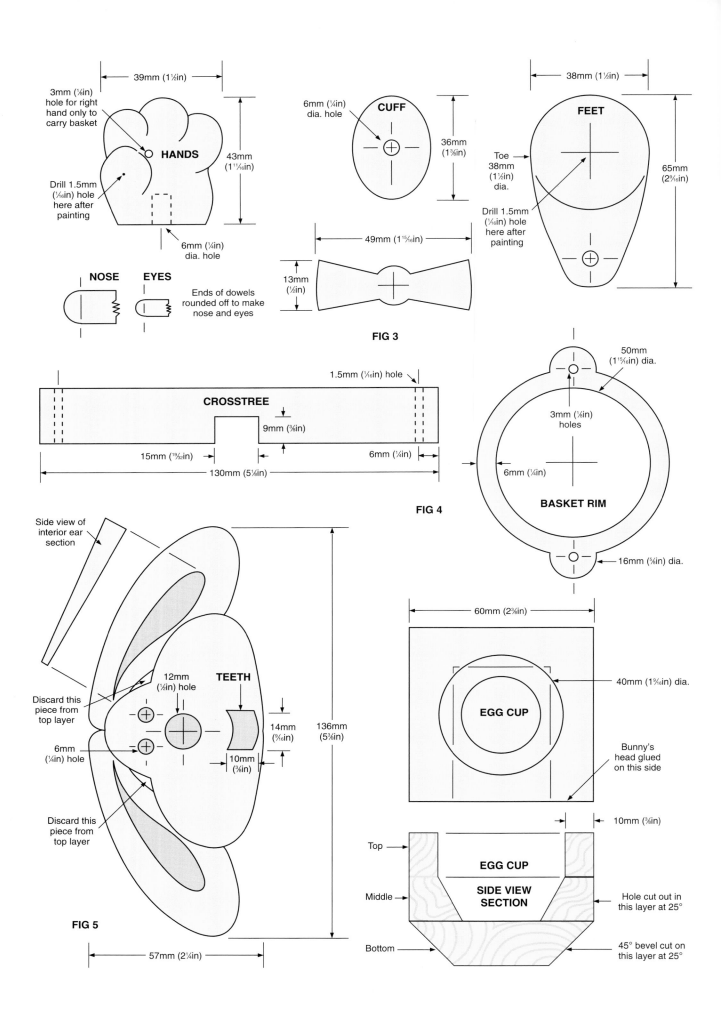

HANDS

39mm (1½in)

3mm (⅛in) hole for right hand only to carry basket

Drill 1.5mm (1/16in) hole here after painting

43mm (1¹¹/16in)

6mm (¼in) dia. hole

NOSE **EYES**

Ends of dowels rounded off to make nose and eyes

CUFF

6mm (¼in) dia. hole

36mm (1⅜in)

FEET

38mm (1½in)

Toe 38mm (1½in) dia.

Drill 1.5mm (1/16in) hole here after painting

65mm (2⅝in)

49mm (1¹⁵/16in)

13mm (½in)

FIG 3

50mm (1¹⁵/16in) dia.

3mm (⅛in) holes

6mm (¼in)

BASKET RIM

16mm (⅝in) dia.

FIG 4

CROSSTREE

1.5mm (1/16in) hole

9mm (⅜in)

15mm (19/32in)

6mm (¼in)

130mm (5⅛in)

Side view of interior ear section

TEETH

12mm (½in) hole

Discard this piece from top layer

6mm (¼in) hole

Discard this piece from top layer

136mm (5⅜in)

14mm (9/16in)

10mm (⅜in)

FIG 5

57mm (2¼in)

60mm (2⅜in)

40mm (1⅞6in) dia.

EGG CUP

Bunny's head glued on this side

10mm (⅜in)

Top

Middle

Bottom

EGG CUP

SIDE VIEW SECTION

Hole cut out in this layer at 25°

45° bevel cut on this layer at 25°

Time to reflect

John Everett

creates a stunning mirror clock that features skills in intricate cutting

This project is probably a little more complex than most for the scrollsaw user and is a useful exercise in bevel cutting, sawing out intricate patterns for inserts and a little wood carving for good measure! Fear not – providing the steps are followed in the right sequence and you are careful with your sawing, you should have no real difficulties in completing this project and will have a new item for your home of which you can be justifiably proud.

The mirror has a scrollsaw surround in which small panels are bevel cut so that the cut out pieces can be refitted leaving a recess in the mirror frame in which separately scroll-cut pieces can be inserted for decorative effect. To complete the piece, a quartz clock movement has been set into the top of the mirror surround to remind those who spend just a little too long in front of any mirror, that time is passing!

1 Prepare the surfaces of ▲ the main sheet of wood – MDF, ply or whatever you have chosen to use for the purpose. Sand it off smooth, finishing with a fine grade of sandpaper to leave a fully finished surface.

2 Now make up your ▲ cutting pattern for the main panel and stick it down in position using a little Spraymount adhesive. You can now mark out the starter holes for the internal cutouts. Begin with the clock insert cutout as this is the only starter hole which is vertical.

3 Put the main panel to one side for the moment and mark up the blanks for the decorative inserts. Use the cutting pattern as a size guide and then make up the three pieces of blank into a sandwich to stack-cut all three pieces at one ▼

pass. The wood used for these little pieces is only around 6–8mm in thickness so will pose no problems for even the most modest of scrollsaws. Stick the cutting pattern in place on the top blank with a little more Spraymount adhesive.

4 Next set up your ▲ scrollsaw with a medium-grade blade to cut out the main panel from its sheet. The outer cut is made first as the panel is a little large. Reducing the overall size of the workpiece will make handling the panel easier for when you come to make the internal cutouts. These are mostly bevel cuts at different angles of bevel.

5 When you have ▲ completed the outer cut of the main panel, set up your saw to make the internal cutout for the clock insert. This cutout is vertical and will pose no problems. Check with the clock insert you have to make sure the insert will be a good tight fit once the hole has been cut out.

6 The next stage is to make starter holes for the edge recesses. You will need to use as small a drill bit as you can – one just large enough to

allow your blade to pass ▲ through is the one to use. The reason for this is that the starter hole must be made at the edge of the cutout and will leave a space which will need to be disguised later. If you make a larger hole than absolutely necessary, then the disguising operation will be that much more difficult. For the example shown here, a mini-drill was used with the hole being drilled at an angle to match the angle at which the bevelled cutout will be made – in this case, 5°.

Materials

- A mirror. The one used here was from a 'Pound Shop' and cost – yes, that's right – a pound. It came complete with a pine frame that was really not up to much and so this was removed and discarded – actually, I lit the fire with it. The size of the example used here is 10in x 8in but you can use whatever size mirror you prefer, providing you can obtain a suitable sheet of material for the surround panel with enough material all round for the decorative effects.
- A sheet of wood measuring 375mm x 280mm or to suit your own mirror if you are using a size other than the one given here. You can of course use MDF or even ply if you prefer and decorate it accordingly once you have cut it out. Use a minimum of 9mm (⅜in) in thickness. The one shown was made from 10mm timber which

7 Once you have drilled ▲ starter holes for all three cutout panels, set up your saw table to cut at exactly 5°. This is easy to do by checking the blade against a cheap school protractor as shown in the picture. The reason for selecting a 5° angle is that this will allow the cut out piece of wood to be reinserted into the hole from which it was cut and will allow it to recess deeply enough to accept the decorative insert with most of it below the surface of the ▼

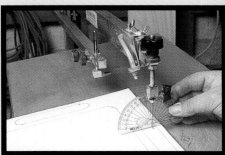

happened to be the thickness of a suitable sheet of wood remaining from a salvaged shelf unit.

- Three small offcuts of wood in a contrasting colour to that used for the main panel. The wood used here was obeche which is a light cream in colour and so contrasts well with the mahogany colour of the main panel. You could always reverse the scheme and use a dark wood for the inserts and a lighter ground.
- Quartz clock insert. The type used here was a type 65CA movement from Yorkshire Clockbuilders. Tel. 0114 255 0786 for a free catalogue. They are not expensive and it is worthwhile using a quality movement for a project such as this.
- Materials for gluing and decorating which will be more or less your own choice as regards finishing your own mirror.
- Picture hanging wire and two rings to fix it to.

main panel. A shallower angle of bevel will allow the insert to recess more deeply into its original hole and a steeper angle of bevel will do the reverse.

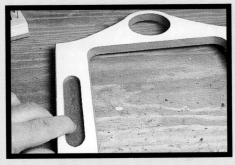

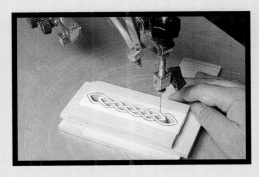

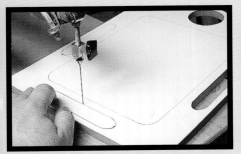

8 With the saw set up for ▲ the 5° bevel cut, make all three of the cutouts, remembering to cut in a clockwise direction or the bevel will be an undercut instead of the correct slope.

9 As you cut out each ▲ piece from the main panel, lay it carefully on your bench so that it is in the same position you cut it out of the main panel. This will avoid having to try each piece for fit later as you will simply lift each piece from the bench and replace it in its original hole in the proper orientation when it comes to gluing them in position. Now reset your saw table to cut an angle of 10° and make the final internal cutout for the actual mirror. The piece of material you remove from the mirror cutout can be reused for something else as it will still be of a useful size.

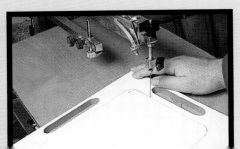

10 The next step is to ▲ refit the border cutout pieces into their original holes and glue them firmly in place by applying a smear of wood glue around the bottom of each cutout and pushing them firmly back in place. You will notice that each piece you refit will protrude behind the back of the panel some distance. Do not worry about this now as you will remove that once the glue has had time to set completely. Do not be tempted to remove the excess until the glue has really set properly as you may well move the insert slightly and it will not remain an accurate fit in its hole.

11 Next take the stack ▲ you made earlier of the three blanks whichwill become the decorative inserts for the recesses in the main panel. Drill small starter holes for all the internal cutouts and make the internal cuts first. Take care to use a sharp blade as pressure on the workpiece to make the blade cut faster can result in an uneven cut through all three of the blanks. This will mean that they will not all match up exactly from where the blade has been bent by the pressure on it while cutting. Allow the blade to do the work and resist the temptation to 'speed things up a little'.

12 Once you have ▲ made all the internal cutouts on the decorative inserts, finally cut around the outside of the stack to leave the three separate pieces.

13 Using the cutting ▲ pattern as a guide, mark out with a pencil on each of the decorative insert blanks where the 'ropes' cross over each other so that you will be sure to make them a matching set once the carving has been completed. Use a small craft knife with a new sharp blade to cut down the pattern of the ropes as shown in the picture and finish off by smoothing away any rough edges that remain with some fine sandpaper.

14 By this time, the glue will be fully set on the recesses and you can remove the surplus material from the back of the main panel. You can plane most of this if you have a plane or simply remove the lot with a sander as I did on the original so that the back of the main panel is flush and smooth.

15 On the example shown here, all the edges were given a scolloped pattern using a mini-

drill fitted with a small drum
sander attachment. If you have a
mini-drill kit you will be able to do
this the easy way but if not, you
can use a file to achieve the same
effect and then finish off with
some fine sandpaper to smooth
out any remaining roughness.

16 Once you have
scalloped all the edges
of the main panel,
finish off by
smoothing all around with fine
sandpaper so that there are no
hard edges remaining. This gives a
better overall effect to the
finished piece as the smoother
'distressed' finish is more in
keeping with the style of
decoration used for the inserts.

17 Next apply spots of
wood glue to the
underside of the
decorative inserts

and fit them firmly in place in
each of the recesses around the
edges of the main panel. Leave
them to dry thoroughly.

18 Once the glue has
set fully, you can add
your decoration – in
this case acrylic
varnish – making sure that the
varnish is worked well into the
tiny apertures between the
ropework inserts. Use a smaller
brush for this to ensure all parts
are evenly covered.

19 Now you can fit the
mirror itself. Use either
the little metal corners
sold for the purpose
or rough up the edges of the
mirror with a small grindstone
(remembering to wear safety
goggles for this) and use epoxy
resin adhesive to fix the mirror in
place. Trim the edges of the mirror
behind the panel with masking tape
much as you would for a picture
frame and trim the ends with a
craft knife to leave a neat finish.

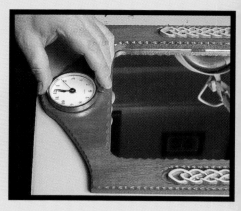

20 Next fit the clock
insert into its recess
in the top of the
main panel. This
should be a reasonably tight fit so
that it will not simply fall out
when you hang the mirror. If it is
loose, you can also use epoxy resin
to fix it permanently in place as
the only access required to the
actual movement will be to
occasionally replace the battery
which has an access cover in the
rear of the movement and will not
be affected by the glue.

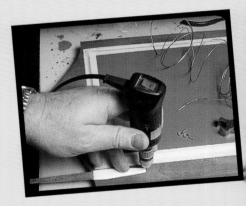

21 The remaining step
is to add the picture
rings for attaching the
wire from which
the mirror will dangle. Make sure
you measure the same distance
from the top edge of the panel on
each side so that the two picture
rings end up level. The checking of
the distance was done here with
just a nail file as a guide as this
measurement is by no means
critical.

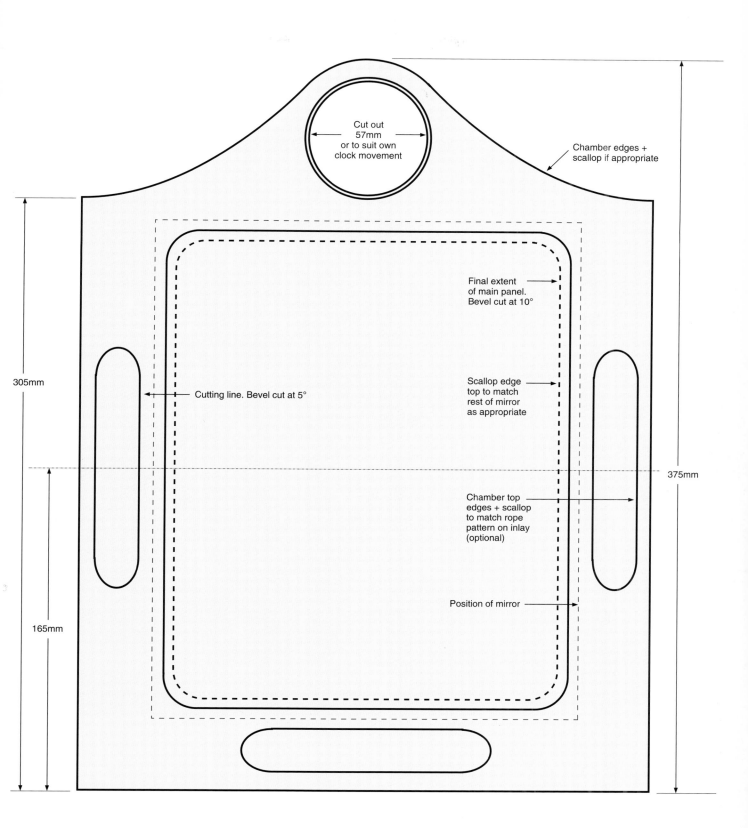

Cut out
57mm
or to suit own
clock movement

Chamber edges +
scallop if appropriate

Final extent
of main panel.
Bevel cut at 10°

305mm

Scallop edge
top to match
rest of mirror
as appropriate

Cutting line. Bevel cut at 5°

375mm

Chamber top
edges + scallop
to match rope
pattern on inlay
(optional)

Position of mirror

165mm

Tied up in Celtic knotwork

Celtic designs are ideal for jewellery as **John Burke** explains

I t all started, as these things often do, with a phone call. My editor wanted to commission me to produce some examples of scrollsawed Celtic knotwork for his magazine. At first I had to think about the kind of project that might be suitable. There are some beautiful examples to be found. Should it be decorative or functional? A complex or very simple design? I would need to do some research on the matter. After careful consideration – about five seconds – I asked how long I had to come up with something. As usual, it was needed yesterday!

Several days later I was surrounded by books, downloads from various websites and believe it or not, patterns from my local tattoo parlour. I found that Celtic designs come in a multitude of forms some too complicated for my purposes, but the main theme came back to a series of interlocking and interlaced knots.

Other designs come in the form of key work which is also associated with Picts, Greeks and Egyptians so the whole idea of this type of ornament goes back a long way. Having researched the designs, I had to decide how to use them in conjunction with the scrollsaw to make interesting pieces for users of scrollsaws, both beginners and experienced. Jewellery would seem to be a good place to start, so I decided on a scarf woggle, as suggested by my wife, using a simple knotwork

design, a Celtic cross using a keywork pattern, and a hair ornament using the same design as the woggle but enlarged to suit the size.

Scarf woggle

The construction is quite simple, two interlocking figures of 'eight' with the ends bent back so that the scarf can be pushed through. I experimented with wood, metal and plastic and decided on brass because the final bending and finishing was easier.

The design was accurately drawn on 5mm (³⁄₁₆in) squared paper, cut out and stuck to the brass plate using double-sided tape. The areas to be pierced out were drilled using a 1.5mm (¹⁄₁₆in) drill to

enable the blade to be threaded and the piercing commenced leaving the outer profile until last. When cutting was complete the edges were finished with

▲ Design drawn out on 5mm squared paper, and stuck to the brass plate using double-sided tape

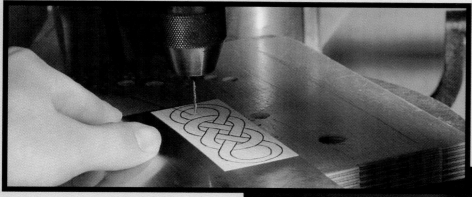

◄ The area to be pierced out is drilled with a 1.5mm drill to enable the blade to be threaded through

▼ Close up of positioning of drill holes

" I was surrounded by books, downloads from various websites and believe it or not, patterns from my local tattoo parlour "

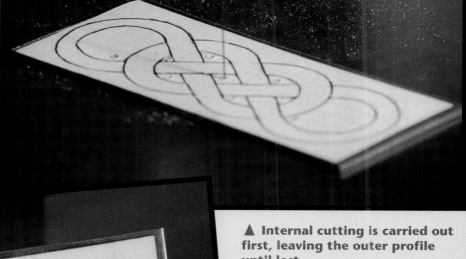

▲ Internal cutting is carried out first, leaving the outer profile until last

◄ All internal cutting is complete – now for the outer profile

Celtic Cross

▲ The impression of the interlocking knot design being applied using a small chisel

Firstly, the design was too small to be drawn on paper so I decided to mark it out directly on the brass, this proved to be a problem later as light reflected off the brass making it difficult to follow the fine lines. At any rate, the surface of the brass was cleaned and I used a blue permanent marker to cover the surface so the scribed lines would show up.

When complete, the areas to be pierced out were centre-punched and drilled 1.5mm (1/16in) in the triangles and 8mm (5/16in) in the four corner cutouts (for the corner cutouts I used an 8mm (5/16in) ground lip and spur drill which cuts thin brass very well, a normal drill actually gives an 'out of round' hole).

The blade was then introduced to each area in turn and cut out following the sequence shown in the illustration.

This cutting sequence enables tight, sharp corners to be formed rather than radiused corners if the work is rotated around the blade. When all the piercing is complete, including the hole for a thong at the top, the outer profile can be cut

needle files and emery cloth to remove sharp edges. The impression of the interlocking knot design was applied using a small chisel, then the whole thing was stuck to a piece of wood using double-sided tape and polished using finer and finer grades of silicon carbide paper (wet and dry) and the ends bent back using a pair of pliers with the jaws taped to protect the brass. The polished surface was then given a light coat of clear lacquer to stop the brass oxidising over time.

Having ironed out a few wrinkles when cutting the brass, to make what I think is a rather fetching and practical piece of ornament, I felt emboldened to attempt the Celtic cross which is quite a bit more complicated.

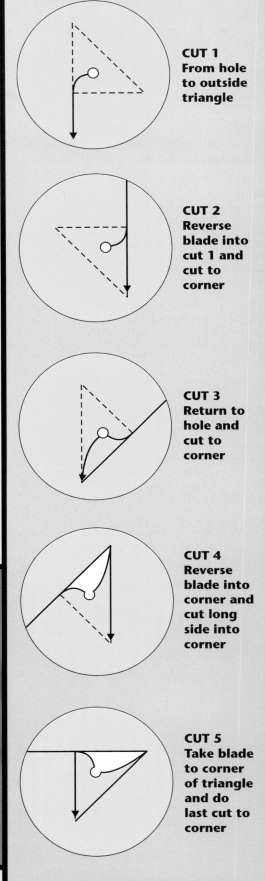

CUT 1
From hole to outside triangle

CUT 2
Reverse blade into cut 1 and cut to corner

CUT 3
Return to hole and cut to corner

CUT 4
Reverse blade into corner and cut long side into corner

CUT 5
Take blade to corner of triangle and do last cut to corner

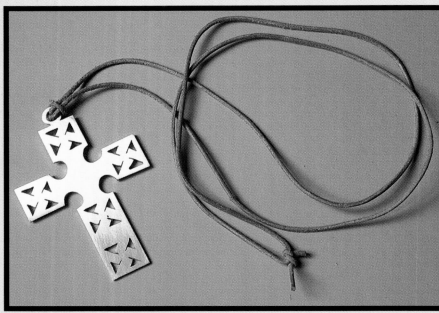

▲ Celtic cross, complete with leather thong

▲ **Design cut out using sequence shown in the sketch. The four curves at the cross intersection were created using an 8mm (5⁄16in) drill. When the cutting is completed and cleaned up, apply a clear lacquer to protect the brass**

out. Any irregularities in the piercing or profile can be corrected using needle files, and the edges and faces can be polished using silicon carbide (wet and dry) paper wrapped around a file. Then the whole thing can be given a light coat of clear lacquer to protect the brass from oxidising.

Hair Ornament

Using the same design as with the brass woggle I enlarged it to a suitable size and applied the design to a stack of 1.5mm (1⁄16in) pieces of ply all held together with double-sided tape. The holes for introducing the blade were drilled as before and all the cutting out done. To finish it and make it easier to use, I

allowed one of the cut out pieces to soak in boiling water for about five minutes and then bent it around a jam jar, securing it in place with string. The ply was then dried in the microwave set to defrost for about five minutes. The curve was then set. The interlock pattern can then be applied using pyrography or a felt tip pen, and the completed ornament finished with

a coat of lacquer. The securing pin can be a piece of dowel or another piece of 1.5mm (1⁄16in) ply cut to suit.

All the cutting out in both brass and plywood was done using my new DeWalt scollsaw fitted with a Neill Tools 44 T.P.I piercing saw blade with the machine speed set to half speed.

More designs can be found in:
Celtic Knotwork Designs,
by Sheila Sturrock.
Available from:
Guild of Master Craftsman
Publications Ltd.,
166 High Street
Lewes
East Sussex
BN7 1XU
Price: £13.95 plus £2.50 P&P
Tel: 01273 477374

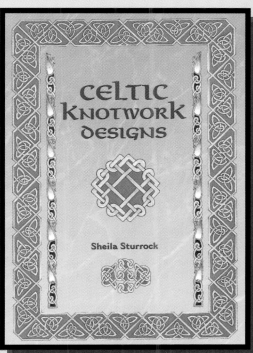

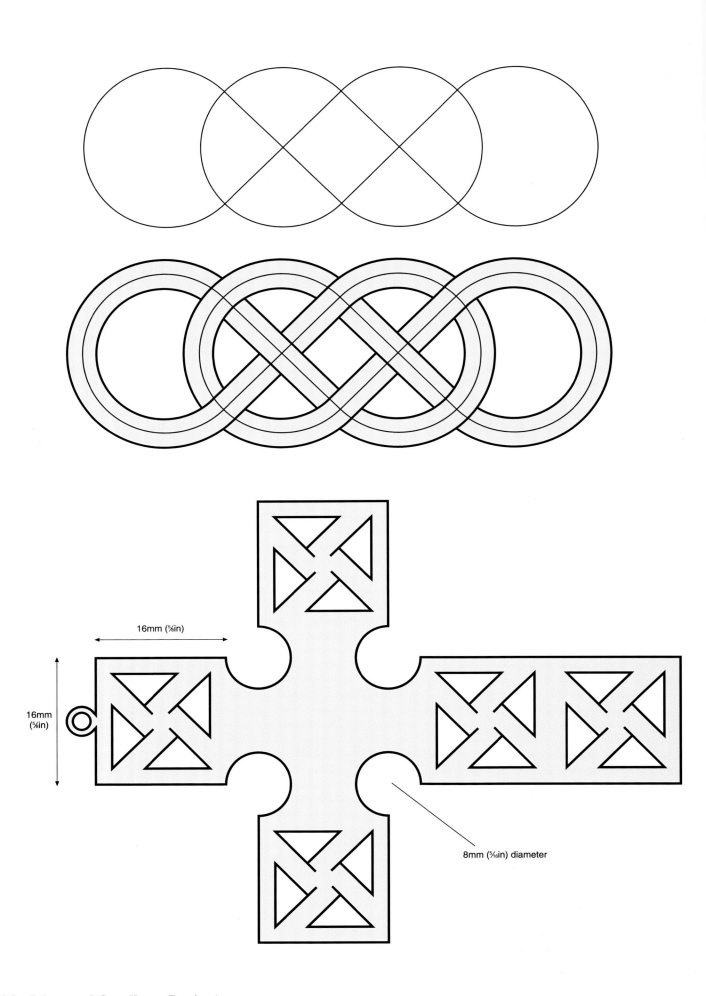

16mm (⅝in)

16mm
(⅝in)

8mm (⅜in) diameter

Let there be light

Traditional 18th-century Swedish style is given a contemporary colour treatment by **Christine Richardson**

This candelabra is made with a scrollsaw and a sophisticated mix of off-the-shelf materials. Everything used is readily available and won't break the bank; assembly is easy too.

The candelabra can be hung anywhere; just screw a small hook into the ceiling at a suitable joist, and adjust the chain for height. On a safety note, do not leave lighted candles unattended.

1 Make a photocopy of the design template, which follows. Cut four of the arms by drawing around this template. Cut one central disc — the centre and each quadrant are marked. Transfer these markings by simply gluing your template to the plywood, or use carbon paper.

2 Fit your blade first in the lower clamp and then, pushing it backwards with your thumb, tighten the upper clamp. Check it is secure and then tension gently. Strum the back of the blade with the ball of your thumb — when correctly tensioned it should sound musical.

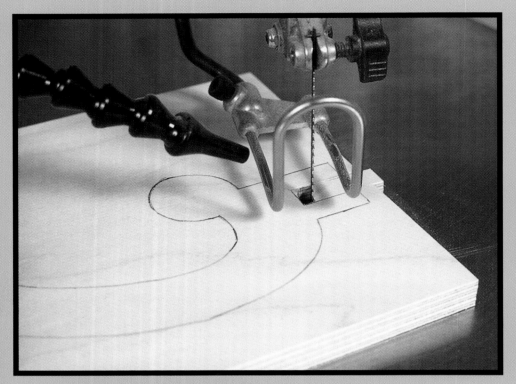

"Placing a thumb on top of the rasp ensures accuracy and prevents flattening of curves"

◄ Make one straight cut to a corner; make a second straight cut to the opposite corner, reverse the blade and leave a small amount of waste in that corner and continue to meet the first straight cut

Now restart the saw and avoid the problem area, leaving a small amount of waste attached to the work, and rejoin the cutting line at the next convenient place.

Materials, tools

- 350 x 480 x 12mm (13¾ x 19 x ½in) birch plywood
- 280 x 32mm (11 x 1¼in) dowel
- Quick-setting wood glue
- Exeter Marine emulsion paint
- Quick-drying metal primer
- 4 night-light candle holders
- 8 x 10mm panel pins
- 1 x 50mm door knob
- 1 x 35mm screw eye
- 1m chrome-plated decorative gothic chain
- Speedline 5tpi blade with return teeth, for timber 30mm (1³⁄₁₆in) or more thick
- Flat wood rasp
- Drill, wood bit and countersink
- Household paint brush

3 Begin sawing out your shapes. Where tight corners or sharp curves make turning the blade difficult, you can either saw to an outside edge, remove the waste and start again at another angle or, *see photo*, stop the saw and gently pull the work towards you so that the blade is taken back a couple of millimetres into the cut.

4 Cut out all four arms and the central disc. If any of your edges have visible saw cuts, or are lumpy from inaccurate sawing, clamp in a vice or to a worktop edge

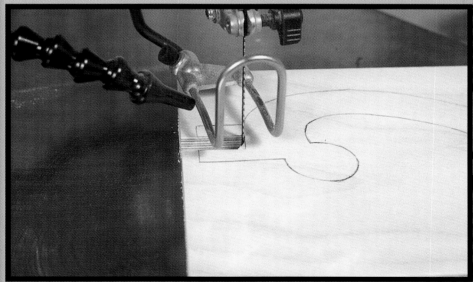

▲ With a large amount of waste removed the final corner is easy to negotiate with the blade. Use the same technique for tight inside curves

◀ **Using the rasp to remove saw marks**

▼ **Central assembly from above, showing placing of dowel and arms**

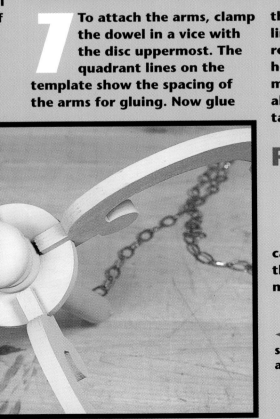

and gently rasp the marks away. Placing a thumb on top of the rasp ensures accuracy and prevents flattening of curves. Sand away any ragged edges that you might find in the work.

5 Clamp the dowel in a vice, drill an overlong hole and countersink for the screw eye, so that all of the neck of the screw eye is hidden. Screw in your screw eye.

6 Next, attach the central disc to the other end of the dowel by screwing through the centre of the disc, *see pattern*, into the dowel. The main body of the candelabra is now assembled.

7 To attach the arms, clamp the dowel in a vice with the disc uppermost. The quadrant lines on the template show the spacing of the arms for gluing. Now glue the arms into position using the lines as a guide, then glue the ready-made knob over the screw head. Let the glue set for five minutes before handling, although thorough curing will take longer.

Finishing

1 Now the candelabra is assembled, remove the night lights from their holders and discard the candle. Paint the holders and the screw eye with quick-drying metal primer. Leave to dry.

◀ **Central assembly from below, showing placing of knob and arms**

2 Paint the entire piece and the metal parts with Homebase Exeter Marine matt emulsion. Leave to dry.

3 Open the bottom chain link, attach to the screw eye and close the link.

4 Use two long panel pins to attach each candle holder to an arm, leaving 5mm of each pin protruding. Push down the candles onto these spikes for vertical candles every time. The candelabra is now ready to use.

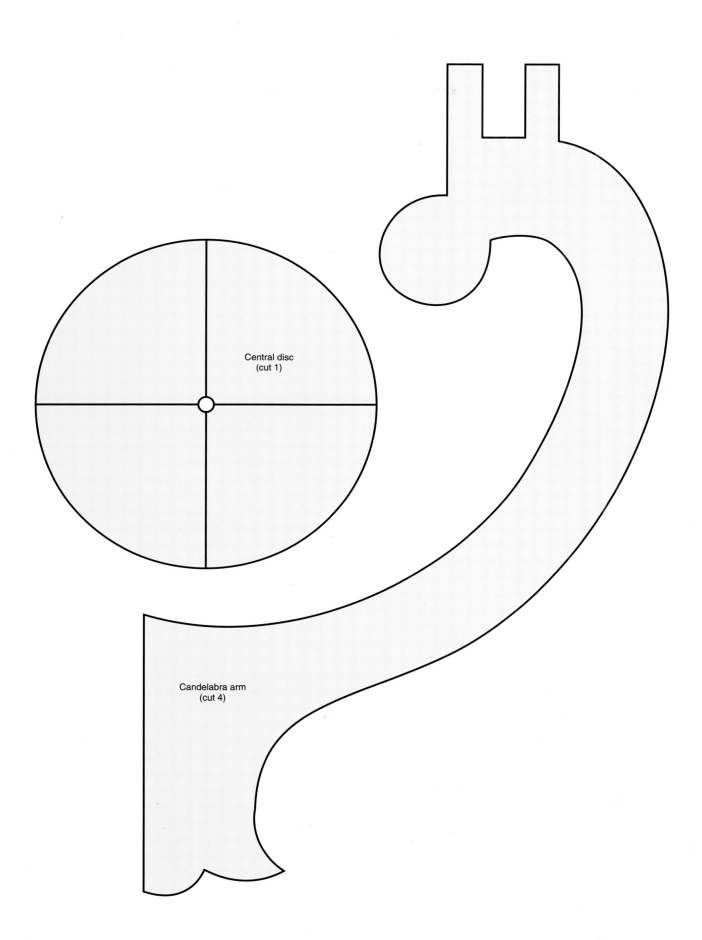

Central disc
(cut 1)

Candelabra arm
(cut 4)

Jigsaurus acrylicus

Little devotees of dinosaurs and whales will be delighted with these jigsaws, cut by **Terry Lawrence** from Altuglas acrylic sheet

Altuglas, a cast acrylic sheet, is similar to perspex, but is easier to work, cheaper and comes in colours that are particularly attractive to children. By way of an experiment I designed and made a couple of laminated jigsaw puzzles, one with three thicknesses of 3mm Altuglas, and one with four.

The dinosaur design measures 333mm by 162mm (13in by 6⅜in) and the sperm whales 337mm by 158mm (13¼in by 6¼in).

Overlays show the exact shapes to cut, and the drawings can be enlarged on a photocopier.

Dinosaur design

This puzzle is made from red, yellow and white 3mm Altuglas. The outline of the puzzle is

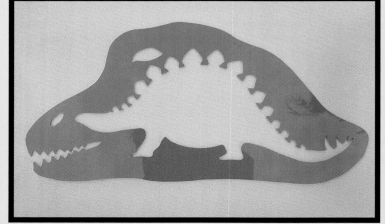

the head of a brontosaurus. Cut into the top red sheet is the silhouette of a stegosaurus.

This reveals its shape on the second layer of yellow, into which is cut the outline of a deinonychus, which shows as white due to the unpierced third layer.

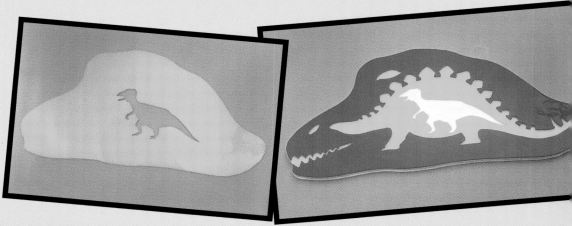

Altuglas is supplied with a protective plastic film on each face, one in clear and the other in translucent blue.

Do not remove this covering until you are ready to glue as the acrylic sheet is easily scratched when being worked. The film also prevents the acrylic from fusing due to friction during cutting.

Using a scalpel, cut out your design from thick paper or thin card, which can be used as a template for marking out.

For the first red layer, cut a piece of Altuglas slightly oversize from the standard-size 1000mm by 600mm sheet.

Lay your paper template on it, and with a ballpoint pen draw the nostril, eye and mouth apertures.

Mark the outline of the stegosaurus in a continuous wiggly line. Three-quarters of the work with this puzzle is concentrated in the top lamination — the rest is easy-peasy.

Drilling

I drilled for the eye, nostril, and stegosaurus silhouette at 550rpm, using a lip-and-spur – brad-point – drill bit, with minimum pressure.

Cut all round the brontosaurus outline and, by threading the blade through the drilled holes in turn, cut out the apertures.

My Hegner scrollsaw has a 14in throat, so I had no trouble in cutting in any direction within the 13in workpiece.

Blow off all the sawdust, place this red piece onto a sheet of yellow acrylic, and draw round it with a ballpoint pen. Again, leave the protective film on both sides. The outline will be about 0.5mm too large, as the pen point will not quite reach to the edge of the red, but this is rectified later, *see below*.

Cut and lay on the yellow piece the template of the little deinonychus,

ensuring that it is placed clear of the stegosaurus outline. Drill within this area, cut out the deinonychus, and, of course, the outline of the yellow acrylic to match the red one.

Finally, and again using the red piece, draw its outline on a sheet of white acrylic, and cut this out.

Gluing

Check that you have clean, unraised edges to all the cut-outs — mine were perfectly flat with the No 5 blade — and, using Tensol No 12, glue the three laminations together, having first removed the protective film from the surfaces to be glued.

Rather than roughen the glue surfaces

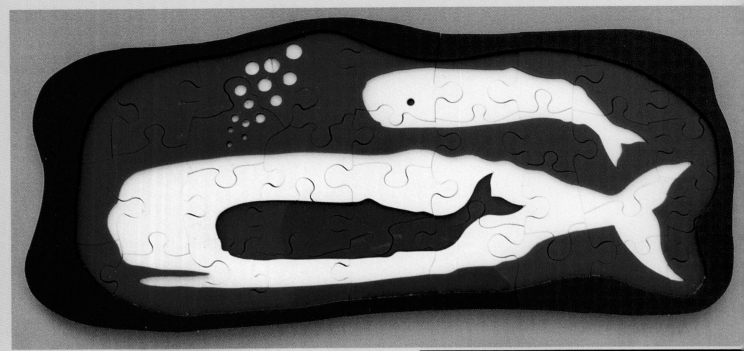

to improve adhesion, which would have spoiled their shiny appearance, I compromised by sanding with 240 grit abrasive cloth the undersides of the red and yellow pieces only, using an old and cheap bristle brush.

Apply Tensol to the whole under-surface of the red piece. Paint toward the piercings, and don't allow the stuff to drip through, as it melts the acrylic.

Check, against the light, that shiny, wet glue covers the surface, then place it on the yellow second lamination, keeping the pair on a flat surface.

Checking that no glue has oozed inside the rim of the yellow surface, glue the underside of the yellow piece, and place it on the white one.

Leave this with a weight on top for at least an hour, preferably more.

Trim, polish

Trim the edge of the whole assembly so that the edges of all three laminations match exactly, using a lathe-mounted flap-wheel or the jaws of a hand-held electric drill. Smooth the resulting edge with 180 and 320 grit fine abrasive wrapped around a piece of balsa wood.

Very slightly round the rim, and smooth by scraping with a scalpel blade.

Polish the rim by either wrapping clean cotton cloth around a piece of softwood and applying acrylic polish No 1, or for speed, using a polishing mop on a lathe.

Cutting jigsaw

Guard against friction-fusing while cutting jigsaw pieces by covering the top

and bottom faces of the workpiece with good quality high-tack masking tape, pushing it into the crevices where layers of the puzzle meet.

Cut the north-south strips before separating each strip into individual pieces.

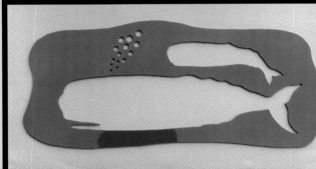

When you have cut all the pieces, remove the masking tape from both surfaces, cleaning the pieces if necessary with polish on a clean cloth.

Check that the laminations of each piece are securely glued. If not, re-sand the under-surface and re-glue, setting aside for a short while.

Whales design

This piece has four layers, *see Layer Warning panel*, including the optional blue framing piece. Cut the other three

first and, if you like the green and white, omit the blue.

The main piece is the top green layer, from which is cut the female adult sperm whale and the albino calf swimming above her tail.

To create the optional bubbles, drill, at low revolutions, with drill bits ranging

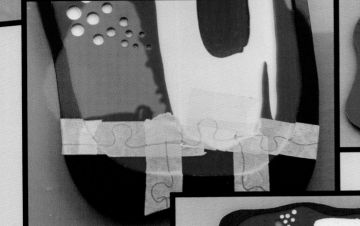

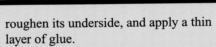

from 2mm (⅛in) diameter nearest her blowhole to 8mm (½in) near the framing.

The second layer is of white Altuglas, and you need to cut out only the second calf within the mother's outline, and, with a 4mm (¼in) bit, drill a small hole for the other calf's eye.

The third lamination is a green unpierced layer.

When gluing these three pieces, roughen the undersides of the top green and the second white layers.

If adding the blue framing piece, roughen its underside, and apply a thin layer of glue.

Cutting of the jigsaw pattern is carried out as before, *see overlay*.

Layer warning

Working with perspex, I found that the heat generated by the blade melted the material, sealing the cut behind the saw blade. If I stopped cutting, the blade would fuse permanently into the perspex!

With single layers of Altuglas, I found that the protective film prevented melt, the sawdust coming off as minute solid white particles. Do not cut more than four layers in this way as, even with masking tape top and bottom, there were signs of melting at the cut, within the sandwich. The occasional scabs of melt on the cut vertical surfaces were removed by scraping with a scalpel without affecting the visible edge.

Altuglas is marketed by Hindley's of Sheffield, 26b Lion Works, Ball Street, Sheffield S3 8DB, tel 0114 278 7828. It comes in 3mm and 5mm thicknesses, 14 opaque colours and seven transparent, plus fluorescents, opal, gold and silver.

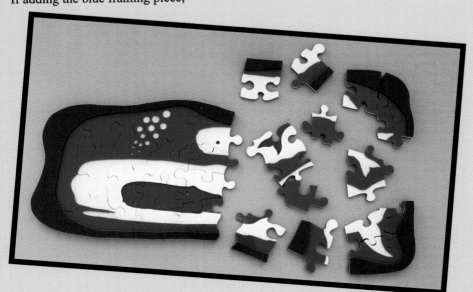

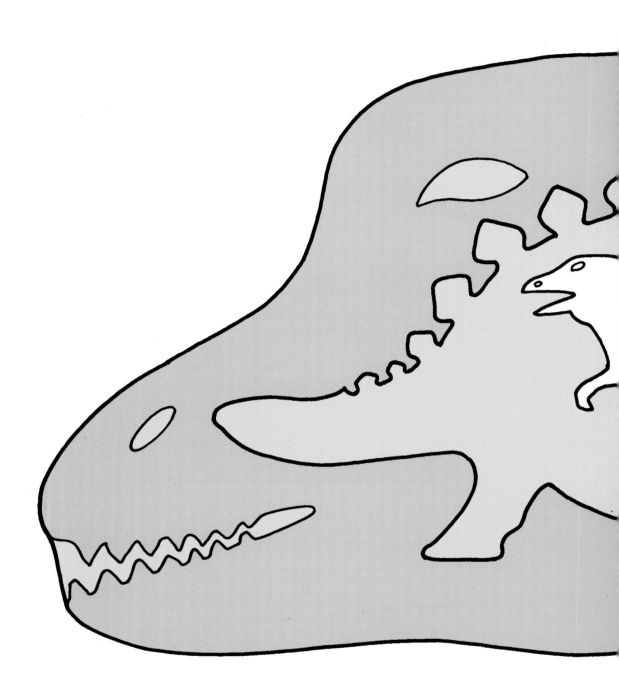

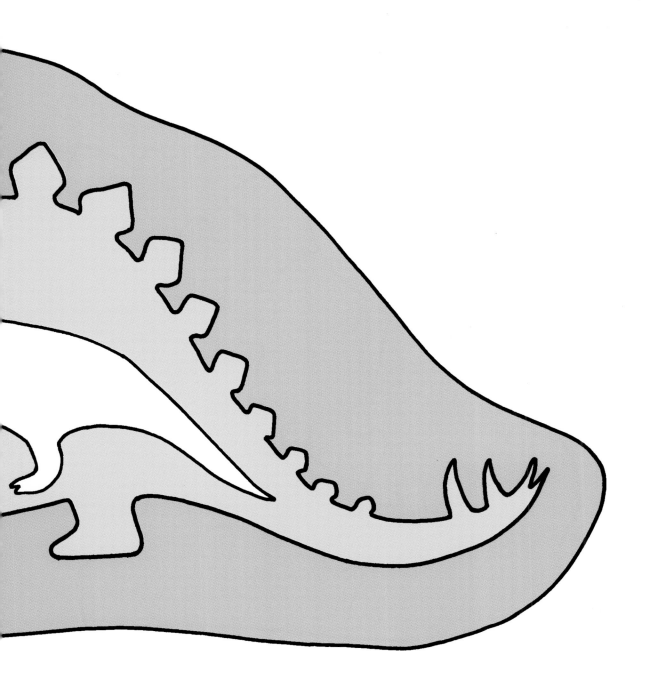

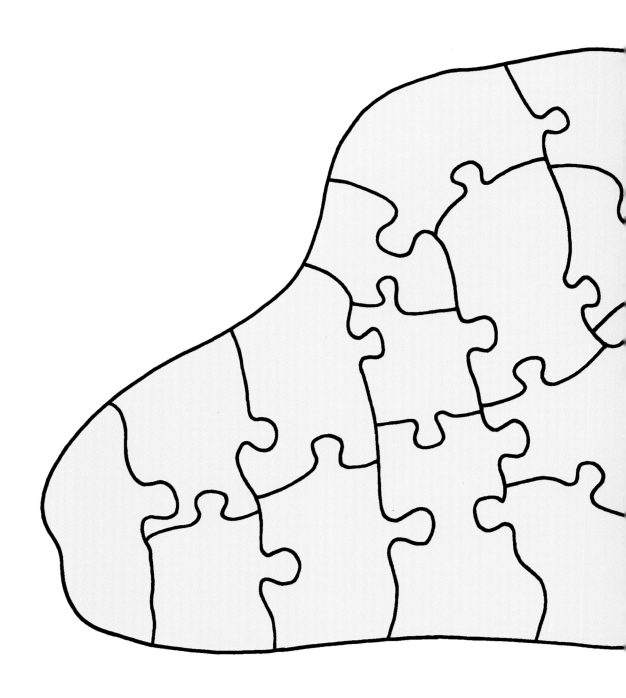

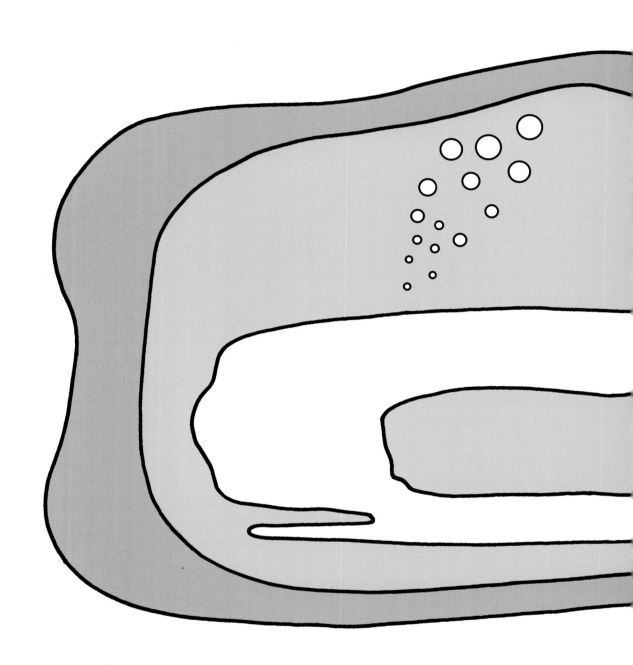

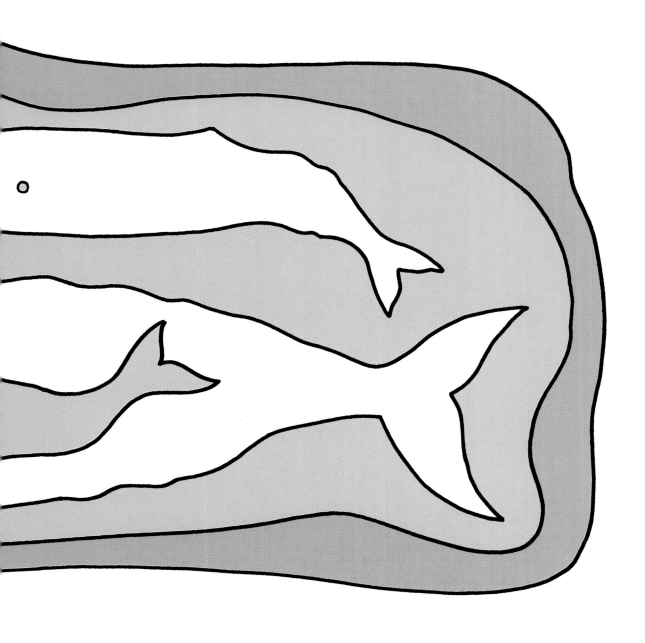

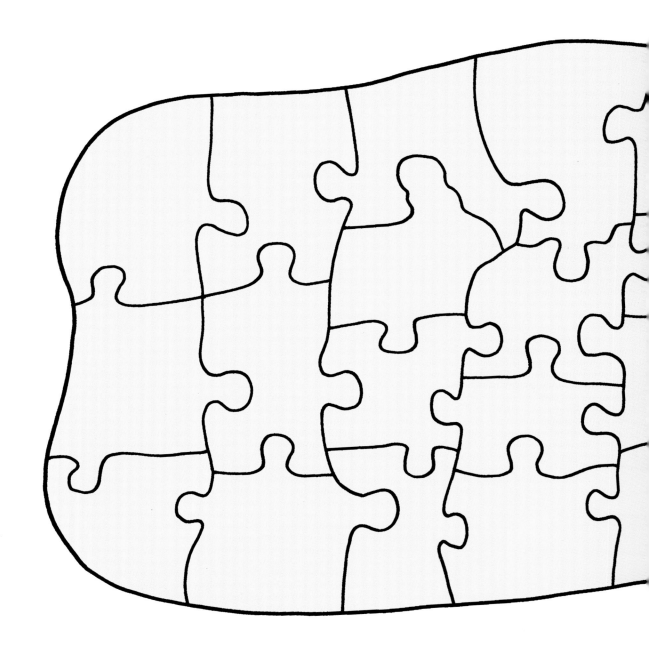

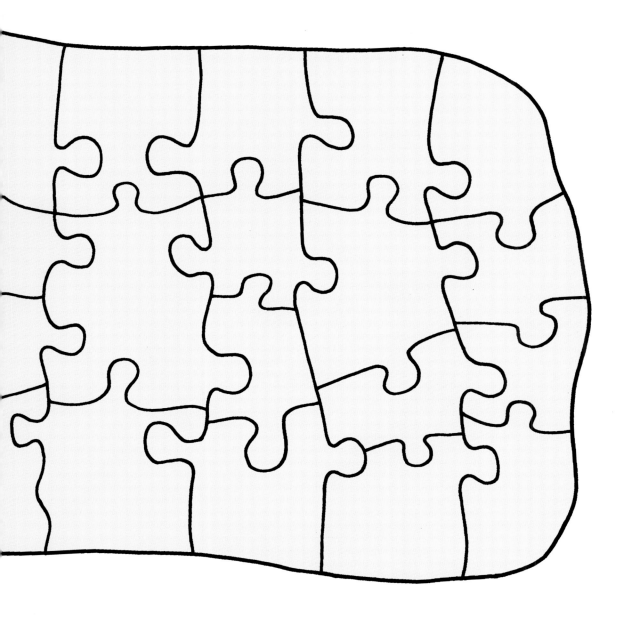

How time flies

Ivor Carlyle brings you Britain's favourite bird as a wall plaque or clock

This beautiful owl which is so symbolic of the British countryside is also sadly much reduced in numbers. I have made two options available for this project, one is a wall plaque and the other a decorative quartz wall clock.

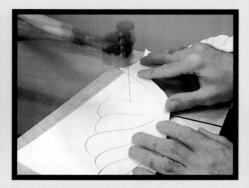

◀ feathers plus the beak and talons. The straighter cuts along the top of the wing for example can be cut with a No 7 blade for speed and directional control.

1 Enlarge on a ▲ photocopier the pattern for the front and stick to a piece of plywood with Spraymount. The repositionable type is best as it is easy to remove. To make more efficient use of the wood I made the wings and the body on two separate pieces of plywood where the 12mm (½in) hole is being drilled for the round eye. Note: if you are making the wall plaque the moon is cut out as a separate disc. The clock version should have the moon as an integral part of the design and cut out as three segments. Also a hole 9mm (⅜in) diameter approximately (check the size of the retaining collar on your clock movement) will need to be drilled for the clock movement.

Cutting list

- 6mm (¼in) plywood
- 1 x front 410mm (16⅛in) x 365mm (14⅜in)
- 1 x backing plate (for clock version) 280mm (11in) x 265mm (10⅜in)
- 1 x moon 190mm (7½in) diameter (wall plaque version)
- 1 x wall mounting plate 37mm (1½in) x 45mm (1¾in) (wall plaque version)
- 1.5mm (¹⁄₁₆in) plywood
- 1 x reinforcement for tail (wall plaque version) 18mm (¾in) x 36mm (1⅜in)
- 1 x reinforcement for tail (wall plaque version) 18mm (¾in) x 18mm (¾in)
- 12mm (½in) dowel
- 1 x eye 8mm (⁵⁄₁₆in)
- 2mm (³⁄₃₂in) balsa
- Small piece to build up elliptical eye
- 1 x 25mm (1in) No 6 C/S screw for wallhanging clock or wall plaque
- 1 x Quartz clock movement and hands. These are available from Hobbies (Dereham Ltd) Tel: 01362 692985
- White acrylic Gesso
- Acrylic hobby paints white, black, silver, gold
- Matt acrylic varnish

4 Round off the end of ▲ a piece of 12mm (½in) dowel and then cut to length to make the circular eyeball on a jig made from two pieces of scrap wood joined together.

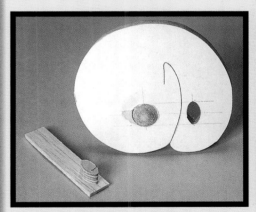

5 Glue a piece of 2mm ▲ (³⁄₃₂in) balsa to the elliptical eye cut out where the round eye has been test fitted. Shape the balsa on the elliptical eye to match the height and curve of the round eye. This may seem a small detail but the crisp, well-defined eyes of the owl gives it its life and 'jiz', as bird watchers would say.

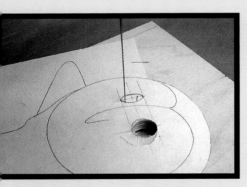

2 Drill a 1mm (³⁄₆₄in) ▲ hole in the centre of the elliptical eye and insert through it a No 2 blade. Cut out the eye.

3 Cut out the segments with a No 2 skip tooth blade. Make cuts where indicated for the wing

6 With a craft knife shape the cuts for the beak on the head as well as for the feathers on the wings and talons on the feet. The cuts

should become the centre for ▲ a shallow 'V' groove that adds modelling to the owl.

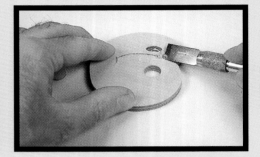

7 Round off the edges ▲ of the segments with a sanding block or if you have it, a mini-drill with a sanding drum.

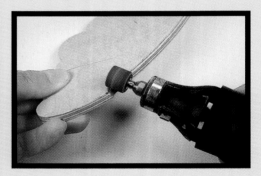

8 Cut out the wall ▲ mounting plate if you are making the wall plaque. The slot which is cut at 45° is best done first as it makes the wood easier to handle. This is not required for the clock.

9 Cut out the backing plate for the clock version the shape of which is shown by a dotted line on the patterns. ▼

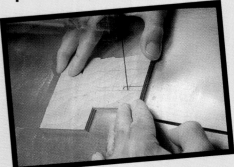

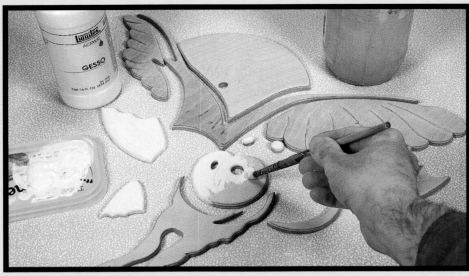

10 Prime the ▲ segments that make up the front. I used white artist's acrylic Gesso. This only needs one coat and rapidly dries. Alternatively any good white matt primer would suffice.

11 Paint the ▲ individual segments with matt acrylic hobby paints where feather details are being added with small blobs of white, black and grey.

12 Paint the moon silver and dapple with gold paint using a piece of bath sponge. Finally, using the sponge again, add a few flecks of white for passing clouds. Note: the three ▼

segments for the clock version and the disc for the wall plaque are shown.

13 For the clock ▲ version mark up the 12-hour divisions on a piece of paper and line it up on the temporarily assembled owl. The radius of the circle should be equal to the length of the hour hand you have selected. Punch out on a stationery punch the little dots for the hours from masking tape. Back the masking tape with non-stick backing while punching. I find the discarded backing from double-sided tape particularly useful for this. Place the dots in position and rub down. Paint the dots and remove the tape when the paint has dried.

14 The eye sockets in the owl's head may need gently cleaning with some very fine (Grade 200) abrasive for the

▲ eyes to slide in Fix in place by applying glue to the back of the head. To give the eyes life and sparkle place a tiny white dot near the top of each eyeball for the highlights. Note that if you would like extra surface protection for the finished project a coat of clear matt acrylic varnish such as Rustins or an artist's acrylic matt varnish made by Winsor and Newton should be applied. Use a large soft brush which should be moistened first to avoid streaking. This is best carried out after the final assembly work has been completed and in the case of the clock before the movement is fitted.

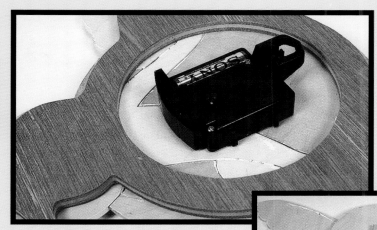

16 For the clock ▲ version, glue the backing plate to the reverse side of the assembled owl. When set, the clock movement can then be fitted. This is a very simple procedure and only takes a few minutes. The spindle is inserted from behind and the locking collar screwed on at the front. The hour hand is push-fitted on and the minute hand is held on with a locking nut. Note: the clock mechanism has a wall hanging bracket built in.

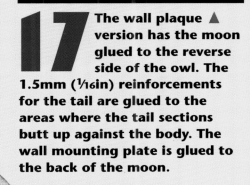

17 The wall plaque ▲ version has the moon glued to the reverse side of the owl. The 1.5mm (¹⁄₁₆in) reinforcements for the tail are glued to the areas where the tail sections butt up against the body. The wall mounting plate is glued to the back of the moon.

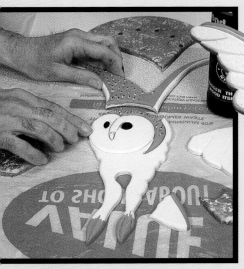

15 Assemble the owl ▲ on a piece of plastic sheet (carrier bag is ideal) by joining the edges together with PVA woodworking adhesive and leaving to set. If you are making the wall plaque version the moon is not added at this stage.

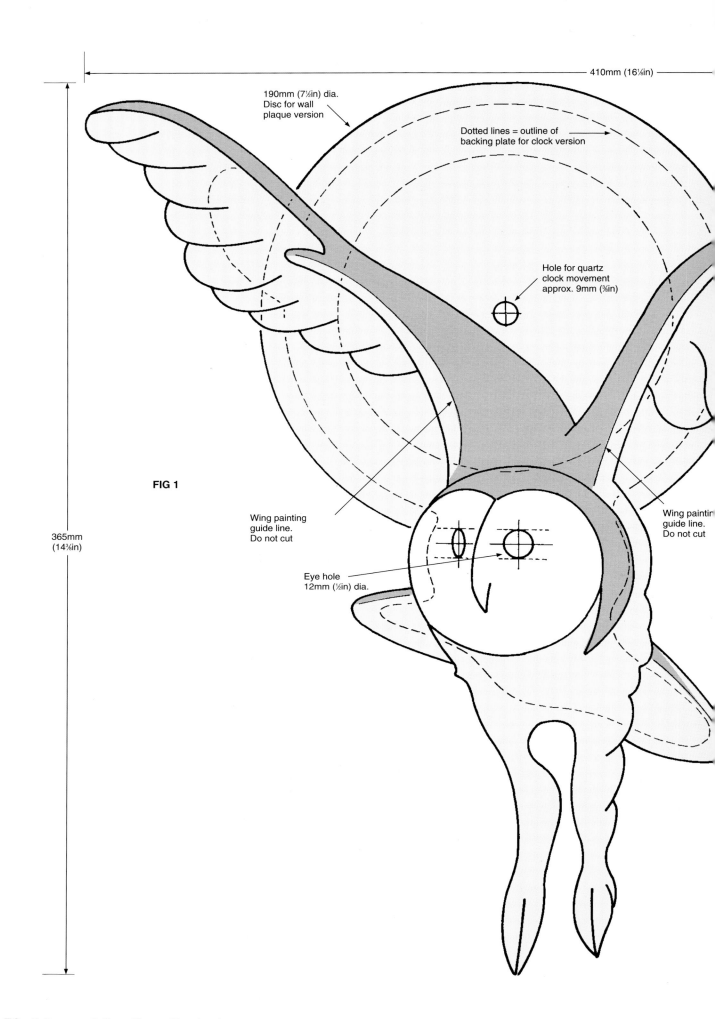

410mm (16⅛in)

190mm (7½in) dia.
Disc for wall
plaque version

Dotted lines = outline of
backing plate for clock version

Hole for quartz
clock movement
approx. 9mm (⅜in)

FIG 1

365mm
(14⅜in)

Wing painting
guide line.
Do not cut

Wing paintin
guide line.
Do not cut

Eye hole
12mm (½in) dia.

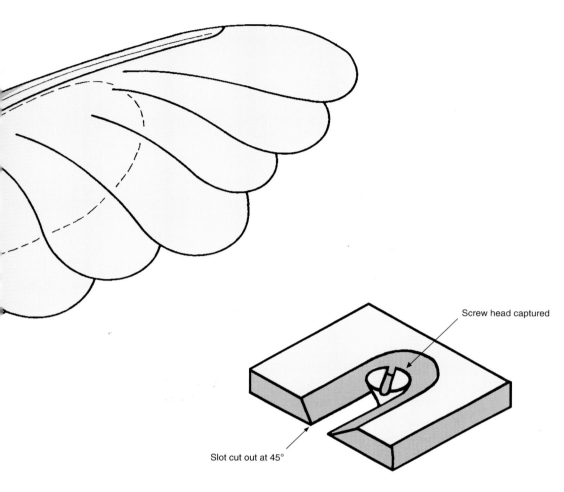

Screw head captured

Slot cut out at 45°

**WALL MOUNTING PLATE
FOR WALL PLAQUE VERSION**

FIG 2

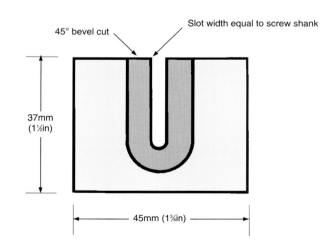

45° bevel cut

Slot width equal to screw shank

37mm
(1½in)

45mm (1¾in)

**BARN OWL WALL MOUNTING PLATE
(WALL PLAQUE VERSION ONLY)**

Part Two
Advanced Projects

All aboard

This beautifully crafted engine design is sure to be popular with train enthusiasts whatever their age
Project and photography by **Ivor Carlyle**

This wonderful Edwardian-style railway engine, is part of a train complete with a set of carriages, people, station and signals, that appears in the authors book, *Scrollsaw Toy Projects*. Railway trains are enduringly popular with children of all ages, especially the old-style steam engines. There is so much you can do with them: passengers need to embark and alight, goods can be loaded and unloaded, there are signals to set, coaches and wagons to be coupled and uncoupled; there is plenty to keep little hands busy. In the light of experience, I have made the design not only as robust as possible but efficient in operation. The couplings provide secure attachment, even across the bumpiest of carpets, and the locomotive can be leant on while it is

pushed along and won't tip up easily. To give the toy a more traditional appearance, I have constructed it out of pine and given certain parts of it a clear varnish. Why not devise your own personal livery? After all, many nineteenth-century railway owners indulged themselves with their full-size 'toys'!

Construction

1 Make a card or paper template of the engine sides (see Pattern 1) and mark out two pieces of plywood joined together with double-sided tape. Drill out the 6mm (¼in) axle holes and fret out the semi-circular holes before cutting out the sides.

2 Glue the spacers on to the footplate, arranging the two smaller sections each side of the larger one to form a cross. Also, glue the bogey support to the chassis (see Pattern 2).

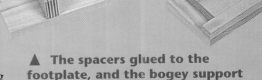

▲ **The spacers glued to the footplate, and the bogey support glued to the chassis**

3 Glue two pieces of 12mm (½in) pine together to make 24mm (¹⁵⁄₁₆in) stock and mark out the wheel arches (see Pattern 1). To make up the two arches, take a 55mm (2³⁄₁₆in) outer radius and 42mm (1¹¹⁄₁₆in) inner radius half circle, cut in half to form two quadrants.

4 Round off the top edge of the cab rear (see pattern 2) before dry assembling, with the footplate and chassis between the two engine sides, to check for correct alignment. Finally, glue together as shown in photo. Tape and clamp well.

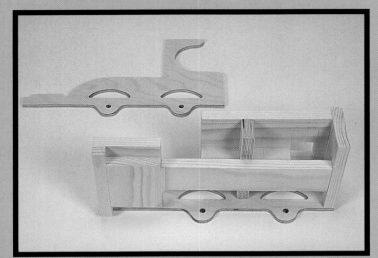

◄ **Gluing together the cab rear, footplate and chassis and the two engine sides**

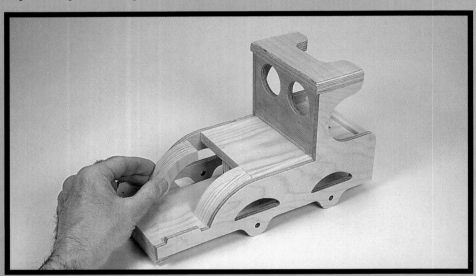

▲ **Gluing the wheel arches in place**

5 Round off the top side edges of the cab roof to about a 6mm (¼in) radius. Glue in place the cab front followed by the cab roof (see Pattern 3).

6 Check the fit of the wheel arches and adjust as necessary, then glue them into position as shown in photo. Sand the footplate and arches smooth and flush with the sides.

7 Glue together two pieces of 12mm (½in) pine to make a 24mm (¹⁵⁄₁₆in) thick front stack (see Pattern 3). Drill a 6mm (¼in) hole in the top for the chimney attachment dowel.

8 Cut out two boiler sides (see Pattern 1). Note how the curve of the underside of the boiler matches the curve on the engine side. Also cut out the top, front, back and fillets (see Pattern 4). Glue these parts together to make the assembly which is being tested for fit in photo.

9 Mark up the boiler block shown in Pattern 4, at the front and also at the back. Check the boiler block sits neatly on the chassis and footplate and check also the fit with the front stack. Any slight gaps can be made up on final assembly but aim for the best fit possible.

10 Place the boiler block in a bench/saw horse type of clamp and, with a balsa plane, plane the top corner edges into a cylindrical shape using the

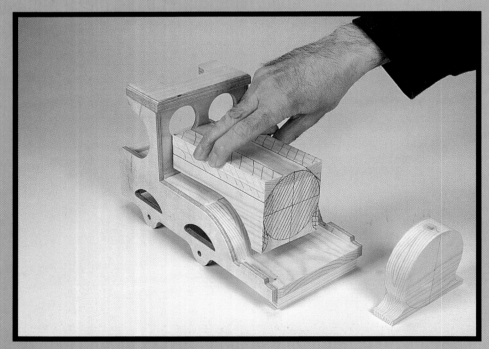

▲ **Testing for fit: the boiler block and the front stack**

◄ **Planing the boiler block with a balsa plane**

13 Glue the buffer plate (see Pattern 7) on to the front of the chassis as can be seen in photo, and glue the bogey support corners (see Pattern 7) on to the bogey support edges nearest the engine sides and behind the buffer plate.

14 Wrap some abrasive paper around the top of the boiler and rub the base of the top boiler dome (see Pattern 5) against it until it assumes a similar curve; then it will sit neatly on top of the boiler. Also, shape the top edge of the dome to about a 6mm ($^1/_4$in) radius.

15 Glue two pieces of 12mm ($^1/_2$in) pine together to form 24mm ($^{15}/_{16}$in) stock. We'll use this to make the drive wheels (see Pattern 8). Select some good hard pine for this job. Also, it is worth bearing in mind that it is much better to use two pieces of pine laminated together than 24mm ($^{15}/_{16}$in) stock, because this makes the wheels less prone to splitting and warping.

16 Glue the 6mm ($^1/_4$in) dowel coupling pivots into the coupling (see Pattern 9). Do not glue the cap on until you have finished varnishing and painting. Put to one side the four buffers

lines as a guide. Hollow out the two concave areas at the front and lower part of the boiler with a small model-making gouge and abrasive paper wrapped around a piece of 21mm ($^{13}/_{16}$in) dowel. Smooth off the boiler with a large sanding block.

11 Drill a 6mm ($^1/_4$in) hole in the bottom of the chimney (see Pattern 5). Note the curve at the bottom of the chimney. To obtain this curve, wrap some abrasive paper around the top of the front stack and rub it against the bottom of the chimney. Join and glue the chimney to the matching hole in the top of the front stack with a piece of 6mm ($^1/_4$in) dowel. Round off the leading edge of the boiler front (see Pattern 5) to about 6mm ($^1/_4$in) radius

and glue it to the front stack. Glue on also the inspection hatch (see Pattern 5) and the chimney top, as shown in photo. Glue the boiler block in place using the front stack as a temporary guide to alignment. Keep the front stack separate until after painting.

12 Glue onto the bottom of the chassis the bogey axle supports (see Pattern 6), coupling mount (see pattern 3) and axle support plates (see Pattern 7) while temporarily inserting 6mm ($^1/_4$in) dowels to ensure correct alignment. Cut out the axle cover plate (see Pattern 7) and temporarily place in position over the axle support plates and drill the 3mm ($^1/_8$in) pilot holes for the locating screws.

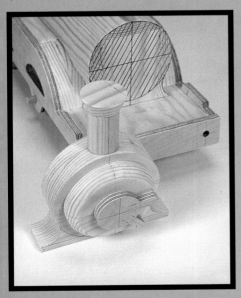

▲ **The front stack with chimney, boiler front and inspection hatch**

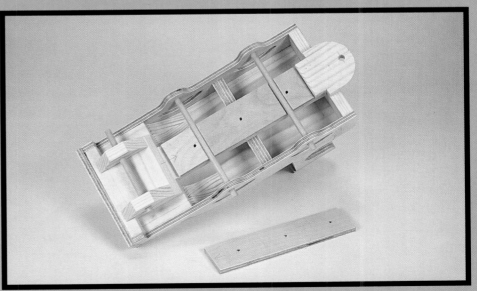

▲ **Gluing the bogey axle supports, coupling mount and axle support plates in position, with the axles fitted to aid alignment**

and the two coupling caps, all of which are identical, until after painting.

17 After you have varnished the drive wheels, make a card template from Pattern 8 and use this as a guide to locate the centres of the black spoke markings. These circles are filled in with paint. Do not cut or drill out these holes; they are too tempting to little fingers which may then be 'guillotined' as the wheel turns.

18 After varnishing and painting is complete, use epoxy resin to fix on the front stack assembly and the boiler dome between the front stack and the cab front. Then attach the coupling – put the shorter pivot through the coupling mount, placing a washer between them, and glue on the cap.

19 Insert a 6mm (¹/₄in) drill into the holes in the buffer plate and extend the holes until they are about 14mm (⁹/₁₆in) deep. Glue the buffer shaft into the buffer, then place a rubber tap washer on to the shaft and stick that to the buffer. Insert the buffer shaft into the hole and stick the other side of the washer to the buffer plate. Do not glue the shaft into the hole in the buffer plate. There should be a gap between the end of the shaft and the bottom of the hole. This allows shaft movement when the rubber washer is compressed due to frontal impacts.

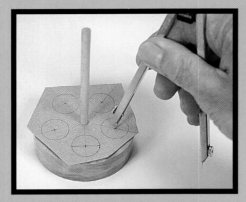

▲ **Using a template to locate the centres of the black spoke markings on the drive wheels**

20 Assemble the drive wheels, axles and wheel washers as shown. Note that the 6mm (¹/₄in) plywood wheel washers are on the inside and that the 6mm (¹/₄in) steel washers are placed between the drive wheels and the engine sides. When everything is in place attach the axle cover plate with screws.

21 Slide the 6mm (¹/₄in) steel axle rod into the bogey axle supports and put the bogey wheels on to it. Place 6mm (¹/₄in) steel washers on both sides of the wheels. Fit a spring cap on to one end of the rod and then slide on the wheels and the washers (the washers go between the wheel and the wheel strut). Before adding the next spring cap, trim the axle to length as necessary, leaving just enough room

for the spring cap to fit comfortably. When hammering the 'hubcaps' into place, use a piece of scrap wood in between to prevent marking them.

Tools

- Scrollsaw
- Blades:
  Grade 0, 25tpi
  Grade 7, reverse cut
  Machine coping blade, 11tpi
- 6mm (¹/₄in) birch multiply
- 12mm (¹/₂in) and 24mm (¹⁵/₁₆in) pine
- 6mm (¹/₄in) and 21mm (¹³/₁₆in) dowel
- Drill, preferably with stand
- Lip and spur drill bits
- Balsa plane
- Small hammer
- Small model-making gouge
- G-clamp
- Aluminium oxide paper grades 100 to 220
- Screwdriver and screws
- Epoxy resin where specified
- PVA glue

Finishing

- Small tins of non-toxic enamels in your choice of colours
- Craft paint brushes in various sizes

Prepare surfaces with 200–220 grade aluminium oxide paper. Vacuum away dust and wipe down sanded, painted surfaces between coats, with a rag dampened with white spirit. For a natural finish, use acrylic varnish.

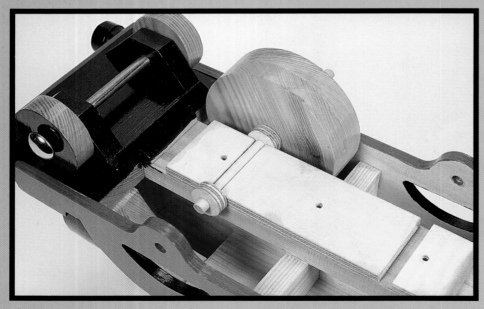

▲ **Assembling the drive wheels, axles and wheel washers**

CUTTING LIST

Item	Material	Size in mm	Size in inches
Engine sides (2)	6mm (¼in) plywood	250 x 144mm	9¹³⁄₁₆ x 5²³⁄₃₂in
Cab front (1)	6mm (¼in) plywood	102 x 76mm	4 x 3in
Inspection hatch (1)	6mm (¼in) plywood	32 x 45mm	1¼ x 1¾in
Axle support plate back (1)	6mm (¼in) plywood	38 x 25mm	1½ x 1in
Axle support plate centre (1)	6mm (¼in) plywood	38 x 82mm	1½ x 3⁹⁄₃₂in
Axle support plate front (1)	6mm (¼in) plywood	38 x 33mm	1½ x 1⁹⁄₃₂in
Axle cover plate (1)	6mm (¼in) plywood	38 x 153mm	1½ x 6in
Buffer plate (1)	6mm (¼in) plywood	114 x 26mm	4½ x 1in
Bogey support corners (2)	6mm (¼in) plywood	12mm square	½in square
Wheel washers (4)	6mm (¼in) plywood	18mm diameter	11/16in diameter
Chassis (1)	12mm (½in) pine	238 x 102mm	9⅜ x 4in
Footplate (1)	12mm (½in) pine	131 x 102mm	5⁵⁄₃₂ x 4in
Bogey support (1)	12mm (½in) pine	70 x 102mm	2¾ x 4in
Bogey axle supports (2)	12mm (½in) pine	19 x 56mm	¾ x 2⁵⁄₁₆in
Spacer (1)	12mm (½in) pine	102 x 27mm	4 x ¹¹⁄₁₆in
Spacers (2)	12mm (½in) pine	40 x 27mm	1⁹⁄₁₆ x ¹¹⁄₁₆in
Cab rear (1)	12mm (½in) pine	102 x 57mm	4 x 2¼in
Cab roof (1)	12mm (½in) pine	114 x 55mm	4½ x 2³⁄₁₆in
Boiler sides (2)	12mm (½in) pine	133 x 65mm	5¼ x 2⁹⁄₁₆in
Boiler top (1)	12mm (½in) pine	133 x 72mm	5¼ x 2¹³⁄₁₆in
Fillets (2)	12mm (½in) pine	110 x 12mm	4⁹⁄₁₆ x ½in
Front (1)	12mm (½in) pine	48 x 25mm	1⅞ x 1in
Back (1)	12mm (½in) pine	48 x 65mm	1⅞ x 2⁹⁄₁₆in
Boiler front dome (1)	12mm (½in) pine	66mm diameter	2⁹⁄₁₆in diameter
Top boiler dome (1)	12mm (½in) pine	25mm diameter	1in diameter
Coupling mount (1)	12mm (½in) pine	52 x 50mm	2 x 1¹⁵⁄₁₆in
Chimney top (1)	12mm (½in) pine	30mm diameter	1³⁄₁₆in diameter
Bogey wheels (2)	12mm (½in) pine	37mm diameter	1⁷⁄₁₆in diameter
Coupling (1)	12mm (½in) pine	53 x 25mm	2¹⁄₁₆ x 1in
Cap (1)	12mm (½in) pine	20mm diameter	¾in diameter
Buffers (4)	12mm (½in) pine	20mm diameter	¾in diameter
Wheel arches (2)	24mm (¹⁵⁄₁₆in) pine	55mm radius x 12mm wide	2³⁄₁₆in radius x ½in wide
Front stack (1)	24mm (¹⁵⁄₁₆in) pine	102 x 82mm	4 x 3¼in
Drive wheels (4)	24mm (¹⁵⁄₁₆in) pine	77mm diameter	3in diameter
Chimney (1)	21mm (¹³⁄₁₆in) dowel	30mm	1³⁄₁₆in
Coupling pivot (1)	6mm (¼in) dowel	40mm	1⁹⁄₁₆in
Coupling pivot (1)	6mm (¼in) dowel	30mm	1³⁄₁₆in
Chimney attachment (1)	6mm (¼in) dowel	25mm	1in
Drive wheel axles (2)	6mm (¼in) dowel	114mm	4½in
Buffer shafts (2)	6mm (¼in) dowel	23mm	⅞in
Miscellaneous			
Axle (1)	6mm (¼in) steel rod	105mm	4⅛in
Spring caps (2)			
Steel washers (9)		6mm	¼in
Rubber tap washers (2)		12mm	½in
Screws (3)	No 6 round head	25mm	1in

**Ivor Carlyle's book *Scrollsaw Toy Projects*, £15.95, is published by GMC Publications Ltd.
Order from Books by Post, 2 Church Lane East, Aldershot, Hampshire, GU11 3BT.
Telephone 01252 331722, fax 01252 318662**

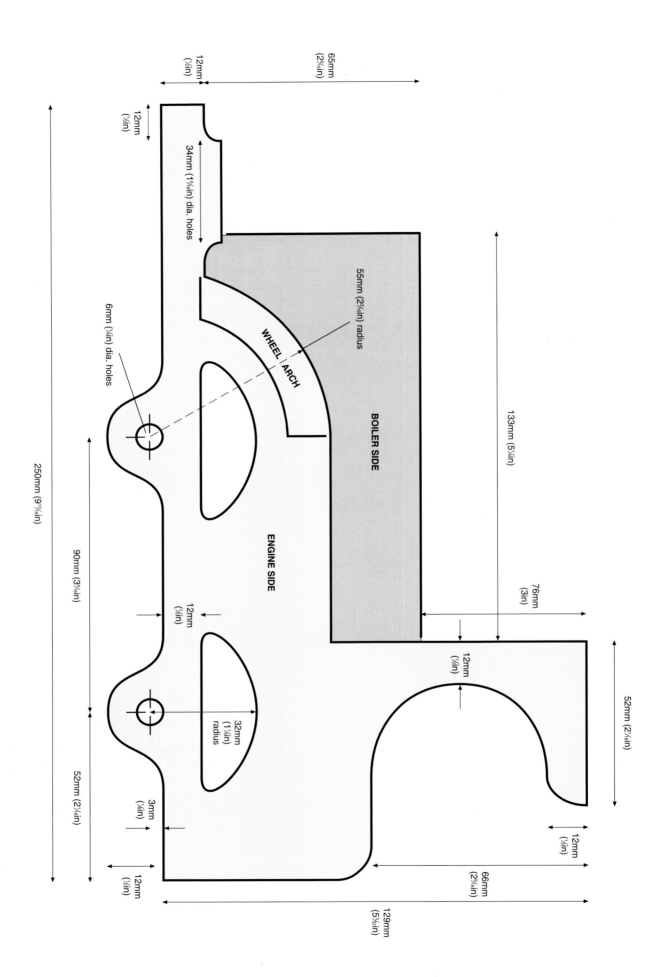

65mm
(2⁹⁄₁₆in)

12mm
(½in)

12mm
(½in)

34mm (1⁵⁄₁₆in) dia. holes

55mm (2³⁄₁₆in) radius

WHEEL ARCH

BOILER SIDE

6mm (¼in) dia. holes

133mm (5¼in)

ENGINE SIDE

76mm
(3in)

12mm
(½in)

52mm (2¹⁄₁₆in)

250mm (9¹³⁄₁₆in)

90mm (3⁹⁄₁₆in)

12mm
(½in)

12mm
(½in)

32mm
(1¼in)
radius

52mm (2¹⁄₁₆in)

3mm
(⅛in)

12mm
(½in)

12mm
(½in)

66mm
(2⅝in)

129mm
(5³⁄₁₆in)

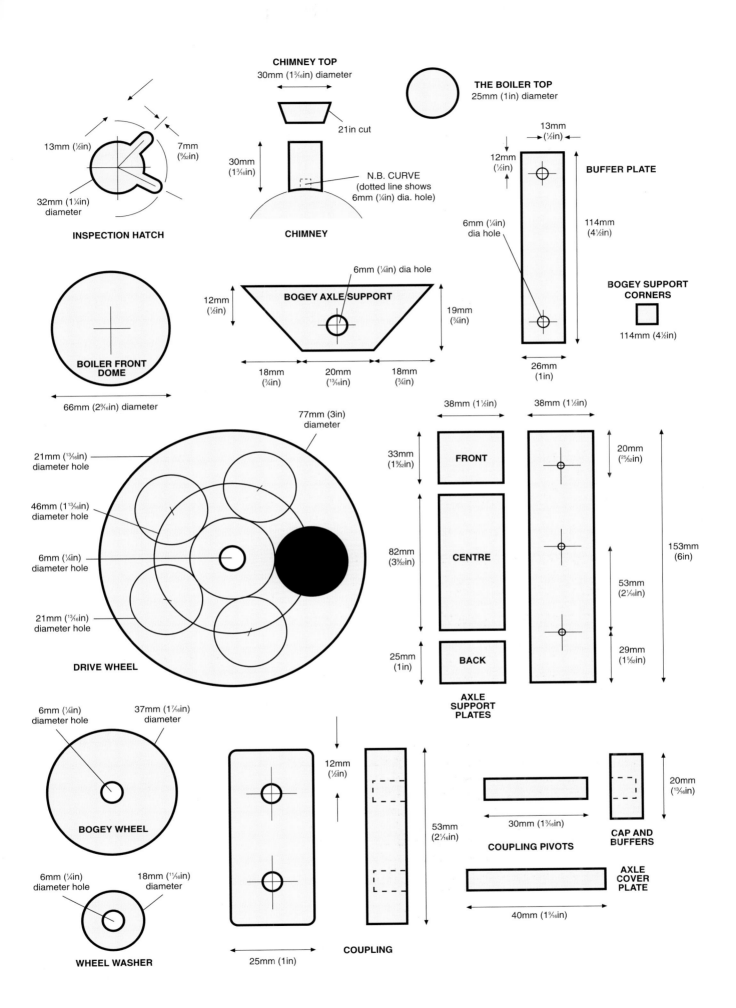

INSPECTION HATCH

13mm (½in)
7mm (⁹⁄₃₂in)
32mm (1¼in) diameter

CHIMNEY TOP
30mm (1³⁄₁₆in) diameter
21in cut

30mm (1³⁄₁₆in)

N.B. CURVE
(dotted line shows
6mm (¼in) dia. hole)

CHIMNEY

THE BOILER TOP
25mm (1in) diameter

13mm (½in)

12mm (½in)

BUFFER PLATE

6mm (¼in) dia hole

114mm (4½in)

BOGEY SUPPORT CORNERS

114mm (4½in)

26mm (1in)

BOILER FRONT DOME

66mm (2⁹⁄₁₆in) diameter

6mm (¼in) dia hole

12mm (½in)

BOGEY AXLE SUPPORT

19mm (¾in)

18mm (¾in)   20mm (¹³⁄₁₆in)   18mm (¾in)

77mm (3in) diameter

21mm (¹³⁄₁₆in) diameter hole

46mm (1¹³⁄₁₆in) diameter hole

6mm (¼in) diameter hole

21mm (¹³⁄₁₆in) diameter hole

DRIVE WHEEL

38mm (1½in)   38mm (1½in)

33mm (1⁹⁄₃₂in)

FRONT

20mm (²⁵⁄₃₂in)

82mm (3⁹⁄₃₂in)

CENTRE

153mm (6in)

53mm (2¹⁄₁₆in)

25mm (1in)

BACK

29mm (1⁹⁄₃₂in)

AXLE SUPPORT PLATES

6mm (¼in) diameter hole

37mm (1⁷⁄₁₆in) diameter

BOGEY WHEEL

6mm (¼in) diameter hole

18mm (1¹⁄₁₆in) diameter

WHEEL WASHER

12mm (½in)

53mm (2¹⁄₁₆in)

COUPLING

25mm (1in)

30mm (1³⁄₁₆in)

COUPLING PIVOTS

20mm (¹³⁄₁₆in)

CAP AND BUFFERS

AXLE COVER PLATE

40mm (1⁹⁄₁₆in)

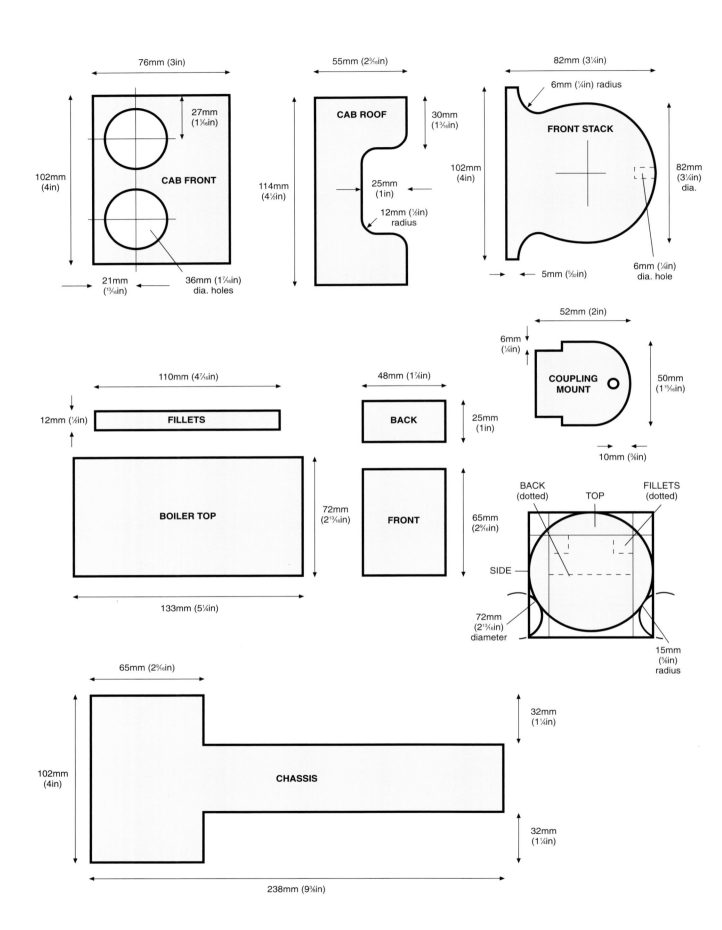

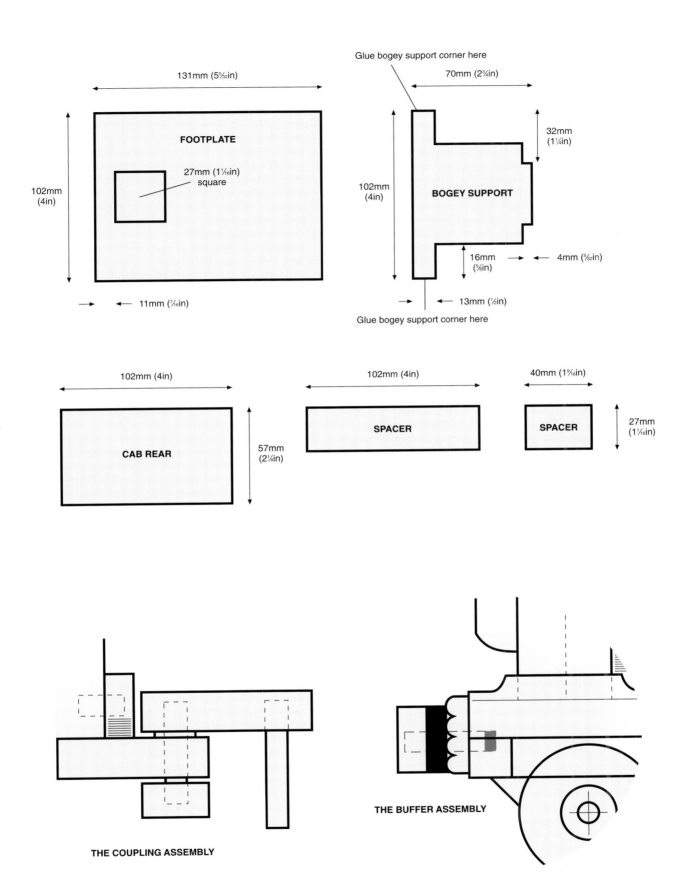

FOOTPLATE

131mm (5⁵⁄₂in)

102mm (4in)

27mm (1¹⁄₁₆in) square

11mm (⁷⁄₁₆in)

Glue bogey support corner here

BOGEY SUPPORT

70mm (2¾in)

32mm (1¼in)

102mm (4in)

16mm (⁵⁄₈in)

4mm (⁵⁄₃₂in)

13mm (½in)

Glue bogey support corner here

CAB REAR

102mm (4in)

57mm (2¼in)

SPACER

102mm (4in)

SPACER

40mm (1⁹⁄₁₆in)

27mm (1¹⁄₁₆in)

THE COUPLING ASSEMBLY

THE BUFFER ASSEMBLY

Ralph Sinnott
goes back to his childhood with this fascinating project

As a boy I used to do fretwork, as it was called then. When I was 13 years old I made a clock calendar working from a pattern given away with *Hobbies* magazine. Some older scrollsawers will remember the magazine and the patterns in green print that used to accompany it. It took some time to complete the calendar as I had only a hand fretsaw to use. When it was finished I stained it, but unfortunately the stain did not take well on the birch plywood I had used. It spoilt the look of it, I lost interest and discarded it.

However my mother kept it and about 30 years later she gave it back to me. I painted it, put the numbers on and mounted it on an oak back board. The remnants of the pattern also survived, these included the date of publication which I pasted on the back of the calendar. Then I hung the restored calendar up in my office where it made a good talking point.

When anyone showed interest I would take it off the wall, show the date on the back and say, "I made this when I was 13". Boasting gets you nowhere; when I was away on holiday someone stole my prized possession. Ever since, I have thought that someday I would make another one. Now, after an even greater lapse of time than that which occurred before, I have at last got down to designing and making a clock calendar to replace the one I lost.

To move with the times I have incorporated a quartz timepiece in the design. Now the calendar clock tells the month, day, hour, minute and second. Of course there are electronics clocks that do the same thing, but they are not as decorative, though they do have the advantage of telling the date automatically. Because my calendar requires the hand marking the day of the month to be moved each day it is best situated somewhere that is passed early each morning, on the stairs, perhaps, or just inside an office door.

"The calendar clock tells the month, day, hour, minute and second"

Materials, tools

- 3.2mm (⅛in) birch plywood 300mm x 380mm (12in x 15in)
- 18mm (¹¹⁄₁₆in MDF 300mm x 300mm (12in x 12in)
- 1.5mm (¹⁄₁₆in) aero plywood 200mm x 60mm (8in x 2¼in)
- Quartz clock movement, spindle length 16mm (⅝in)
- Acrylic craft paints
- Rub-down figures, 10mm (36pt.) No. 1 to 31, 7.5mm (28pt.) No. 1–12
- Spraymount
- Sandpaper
- Drill and bits
- Scrollsaw

Plywood

Birch plywood 3.2mm (⅛in) thick is used for the face of the clock calendar. This plywood is not easy to come by, I bought a 1.5m x 1.5m (5ft x 5ft) sheet from a sheet materials supplier. Though this is much more than I need for the clock calendar it will have many more uses, not all in single thickness, if I want some 6.4mm (¼in) good quality plywood I shall glue two pieces together under pressure.

Small panels of birch plywood large enough for the clock calendar can be obtained from suppliers of hobby materials by mail order. For the backboard I used 18mm (¹¹⁄₁₆in) MDF. If you are fortunate to have a store selling kitchen manufacturers' surplus door blanks near at hand you will be able to buy the MDF quite cheaply.

▲ Pivoting pattern around central screw when boring starter holes

1 Choose the face side of the plywood and stick the pattern to it with Spraymount or Pritt Stick. Saw round the circumference and true up the edge. This is easily done if you have a disc sander. If you don't, you might consider making a sanding disc to use in an electric drill. Cut out a disc from a piece of timber 20mm thick. Take a suitable bolt and cut off the head, fix this to the disc with two nuts, one let in flush with the face of the disc, the other acting as a lock nut. The size of the disc and of the bolt will depend on the machine you are using. For a 13mm (½in) drill a 125mm (5in) disc and a 8mm (⁵⁄₁₆in) bolt are suitable. In use, the drill needs to be held firmly and horizontally while the workpiece is supported on an improvised rest.

2 Drill the starter holes in the regular part of the pattern. This is made easier if the workpiece is fastened to the drill table by a central screw. Once the drill bit is lined up, the workpiece can be revolved to bring the bit into position for all holes in the same ring. *See photo 1.*

3 Drill the starter holes in the remainder of the pattern. If you choose to use a pinned saw blade because of the ease in threading (compared with that of a plain blade), then where there is not room for the normal 6mm (¼in) hole, drill two 3.2mm (⅛in) holes side by side and break out the material between them.

4 Saw out the pattern. Tackle the easier parts, first finishing with names of the months.

▲ Cutting out the names of the months

Pattern drilled to allow use of pin end blades ▼

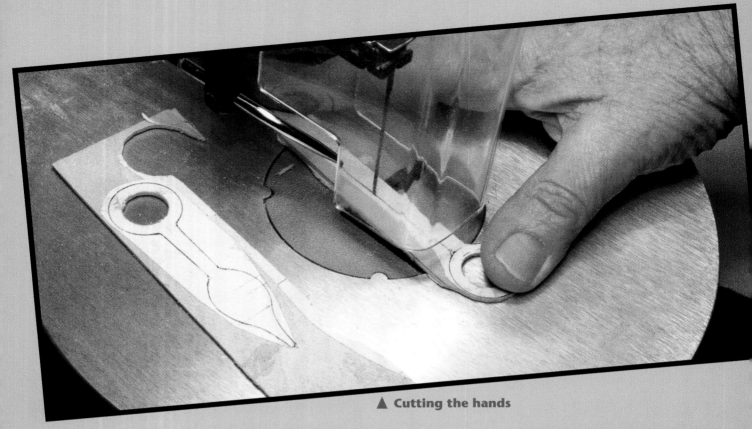

▲ Cutting the hands

5 Cut out the date and month hands and the washers that are used with them from 1.5mm (¹⁄₁₆in) plywood. This is obtainable from aeromodellers shops. As an alternative, make your own by gluing pieces of veneer together under pressure.

6 Unless suitable hour and minute hands have been purchased, cut these from 0.4mm (¹⁄₆₄in) brass. Fasten the brass to a piece of plywood with double-sided tape and use a fine saw blade.

7 Build up the material for the hollow spindle on which the date and month hands pivot from four pieces of 1.5mm (¹⁄₁₆in) plywood. Bore in it a hole of a diameter to suit the spindle of the clock movement. Then shape the outside diameter so the date and month hands fit over it fairly tightly. Glue the spindle in place with PVA glue holding it

firmly for about one minute until the glue grips.

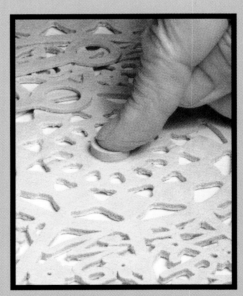

▲ Gluing the hollow spindle in place

8 Cut out the MDF back board and sand the edge. Follow the dotted lines on the pattern to make the cut-out for the clock movement. Fit the 3.2mm (¹⁄₈in) plywood backing piece into the cut-out.

9 Give everything a coat of acrylic priming. Then paint the various parts in the colours chosen. When the paint is dry, carefully spread some impact adhesive on the back of the fretwork, then pin the fretwork to the back board through pre-bored holes at north, south, east and west points of the date places.

10 Make a hole and slot in the back of the back board to receive the screw head on which the clock calendar will hang. Using rub-down transfer put the figures for the dates and hours on the face of the clock calendar. Use 10mm (³⁄₈in) high figures for the dates and 7.5mm (⁵⁄₁₆in)high figures for the hours.

11 Give the clock calendar a coat of acrylic varnish. Assemble the parts.

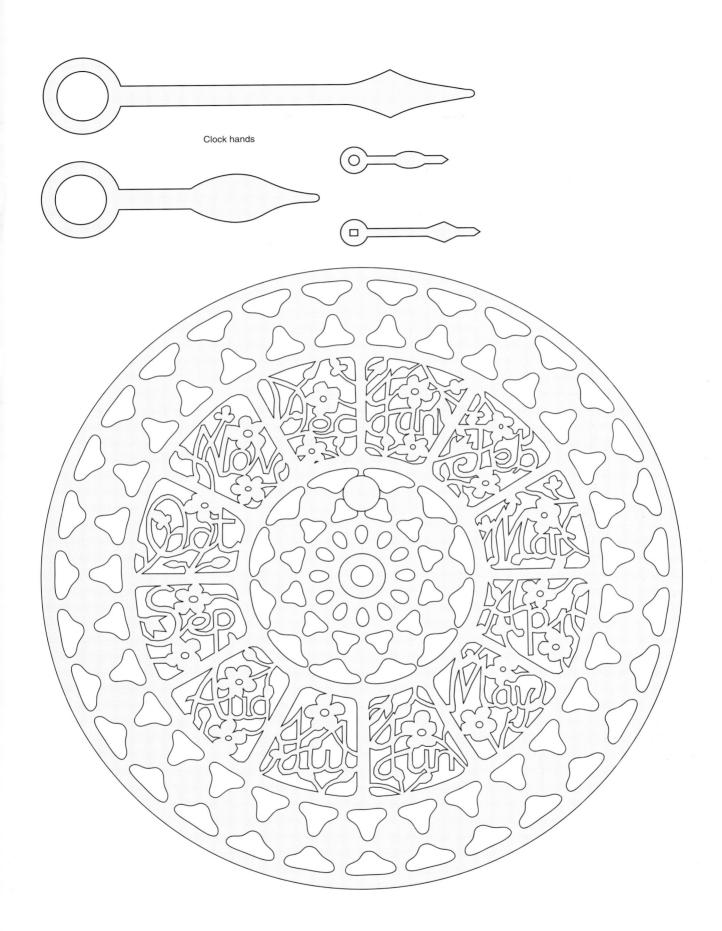

Clock hands

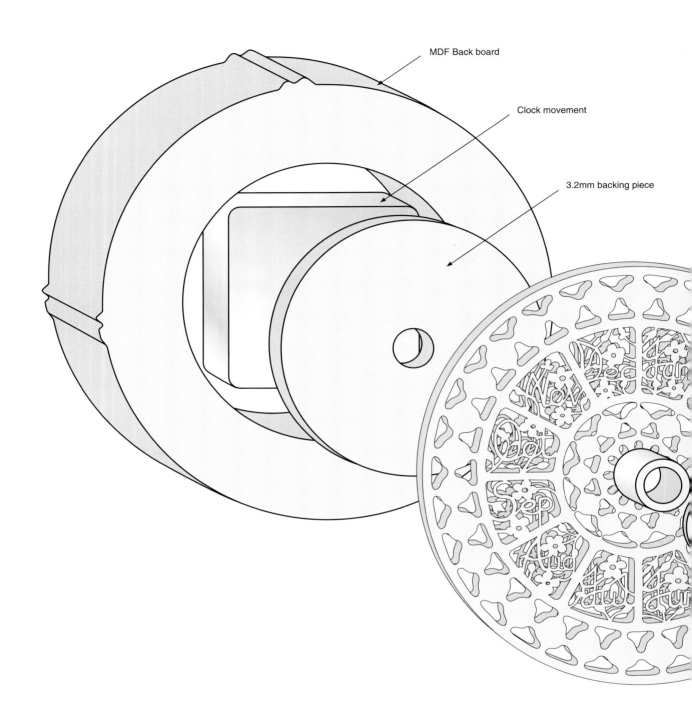

MDF Back board

Clock movement

3.2mm backing piece

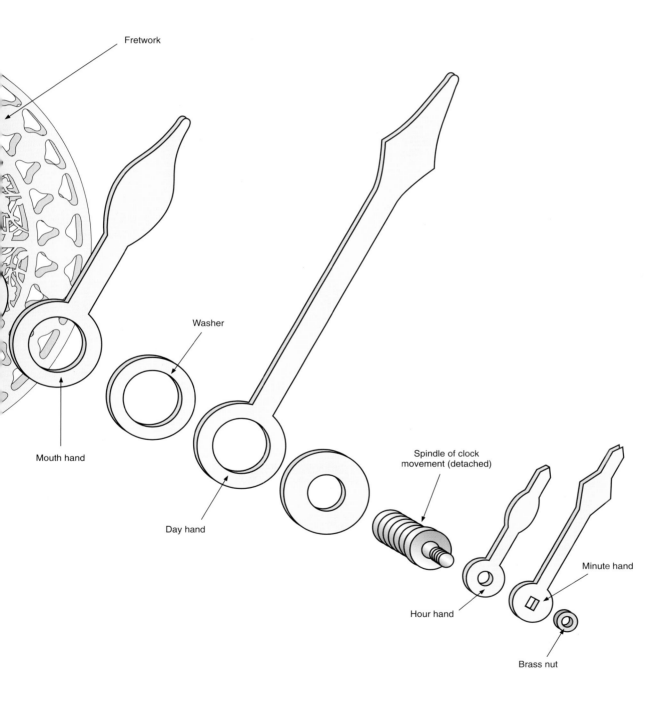

Fretwork

Mouth hand

Washer

Day hand

Spindle of clock
movement (detached)

Hour hand

Minute hand

Brass nut

Vasilissa and the White Horseman

Based on an
illustration by
Russian artist
Ivan Bilibin,
**Terry
Lawrence**
creates a three-
dimensional
picture

I have taken three of Ivan
Bilibin's illustrations, which
make up a trio of horsemen
and have interpreted them as
multi-layered, three dimensional
pictures, ideal for the scrollsaw.
Each layer is cut from MDF (or
you could use birch plywood) and
painted with craft acrylics.

You don't need to be an artist, as
you can trace the drawings direct
onto the MDF using carbon paper.
Just cut around the outer lines,
paint between the inner lines and
assemble. The painting is easier
than it may look, as there is no
shading. Bilibin's drawings were
filled with flat colour between the
lines and you can do the same. As
you can see from the photos, you
don't need to paint the whole of each
layer, apart from the top one.

The first picture is "Vasilissa and the
White Horseman" (representing 'Bright

Day'). The second picture is "The Red
Horseman" ('Radiant Sun') and the third
is "The Black Horseman" ('Dark Night').
Let us start with notes on how to

construct the 'White Horseman'; the
others will follow in subsequent chapters
of this book.

Method

1 Cut six oblongs of 4mm thick MDF, each 260mm x 340mm (10⅜in 13⅜in). (6mm (¼in) is too thick and clumsy; 2mm (⁵⁄₆₄in) is too weak.)

2 Enlarge by photocopier the drawings given at the centre of this magazine to equal the above measurements. You can, of course, make your picture larger or smaller than mine, by using a different enlargement factor.

3 For the top layer, the one with Vasilissa looking into the forest, transfer the drawing to the sheet of MDF (or ply) by using carbon paper. I hold the drawing, with carbon paper beneath it face down, temporarily with masking tape. I use a blue ball-point pen to trace the pattern; it gives a strong fine line and you can see by the blue line how far you have got. I prefer to trace only the cutting lines at this stage and I add the internal painting lines later, after the cut MDF has been sanded on both faces.

4 Cut the outline using a fine blade. I use a No 0 or No 1 for this fine work. If you have a variable speed saw, you will find the slow speed very helpful when cutting fine detail. This was the first project on my new Record 20 saw and the slowest speed of 300 rpm was a blessing; almost like hand-cutting!

5 Drill holes for each of the piercings. There are 25 of these on the top sheet and most can be drilled with a 3mm bit. Use a smaller bit for the tiny ones.
When you have finished the

First layer, cut from 4mm MDF

cutting, sand both top and bottom faces on a belt sander, or by hand with a block wrapped with, say, 240 grit abrasive.

6 Continue by cutting sheets 2–5. The sixth sheet is left uncut and will have a bit of sky painted later on its top left-hand corner.

7 Assemble the sheets in order and you will clearly see where support will be needed; under the left-hand tree trunk, under Vasilissa and under the top of the right-hand tree trunk. Little bits of scrap 4mm (⁵⁄₃₂in) MDF can be cut and glued to sheet No 3 for this purpose, before painting. Superglue is fine for this and is ready in 10 seconds.

Painting

Materials

- One sheet 4mm (⁵⁄₃₂in) MDF 1220mm x 610mm (4ft x 2ft)
- One piece 6mm (¼in) MDF 344mm x 424mm (13½in x 16½in)
- Craft acrylic paints
- Carbon paper for tracing
- Fine drawing pen (Edding Profilpen 1800, 0.1mm)

I

First layer, painted

used craft acrylics throughout, apart from the first treatment of the frame. These paints are about one pound for a 2oz bottle and are therefore very economical. My local art shop stocks 50 shades, so you don't need to do much mixing, unless you want to.

First trace the internal lines onto the cut MDF sheet, making sure that the drawing is aligned with the cut outline. My photos of the painted layers will guide you as to colours. You don't need to paint the cut edges, just the top face of the MDF. I used only two brushes: Prolene artists brushes, sizes No 0 and No 3.

The carboned lines may just show through the paint, especially through the lighter colours. This is an advantage, as your final process, when the paint is fully dry, is to emphasise these lines in black. For this, I used an Edding drawing pen with the finest (0.1mm) tip. Don't press hard, and store the pen with its cap on, point down, to allow the ink to flow when used.

If you mark sheets 2–6 in pencil to show the extent of the sheet above it, you will see that only the bits which will show in the finished picture need to be painted. As an example, in the fourth sheet, only the horseman and the front of the horse need to be painted, as the foliage of the third sheet covers the rest.

Frame

This is in three pieces; an oblong box, an overlapping flat plate with cut-out and a fretted overlay.

Second layer, cut   Second layer, painted

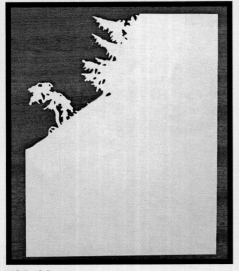

Third layer, cut   Third layer, painted
                           (Note the four supports for parts of the
                           second layer)

3 The fretwork overlay has the same external dimensions as this 6mm (¼in) plate, but is only 35mm wide. I was able to cut the pattern in this overlay in one piece, but if your scrollsaw throat is too small, you can cut the elements separately (top, bottom and sides) and glue them in place later, butting up to one another.

4 The fret is a simple pattern of stylised fir trees top and bottom. The left and right verticals contain ravens perched on trees. When cut and sanded, glue this fretting to the 6mm (¼in) MDF frame plate. I found it easiest to stain this frame top assembly (Chestnut wood stain, 50% green 50% yellow). You should stain the cut edges of the fretting as well as the base surface between frets and also stain the edges of the frame. Just leave the back under-surface plain, as you will glue this later to the softwood box frame.

5 It is easiest to paint the pattern on the frame before final assembly; trees mid-green, ravens charcoal grey (not black) with yellow beaks and white eyes, top frame lines magenta.

1 Make up a box to contain the six picture layers (including the uncut back plate). It can be made of four pieces of softwood 24mm x 10mm (1in x ⅜in) with the internal dimensions to accept the picture elements, i.e. 260mm x 340mm (10⅜in x 13⅜in). Pin and glue the four pieces together, checking the corners with a square. I stained the inner face green with Chestnut wood stain (dry in 10 minutes), as the bare wood showed in part on the finished work.

2 The oblong flat plate is cut from 6mm (¼in) thick MDF. Its cut-out overlaps the base box by (⅛in)

3mm all round, to hold in the components and it is 45mm (1¾in) wide all round, giving external dimensions of 344mm x 424mm (13½in x 16½in).

Fourth layer, cut

Fourth layer, painted

6 Glue the stained and painted assembly onto the base frame, ensuring that it is square and that it overlaps the picture area 3mm (⅛in) all round. The layers of the picture, which do not need to be glued together, can be held in place at the rear with nails, cross-straps of 4mm (⁵⁄₃₂in) MDF strip screwed to the softwood, or with a ply or MDF backing plate.

In the next chapter, I provide photos and drawings of the Red Horseman and detail any variations in the construction methods. The methods are similar, so keep these notes handy.

Fifth layer, cut

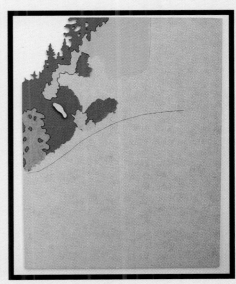

Fifth layer painted

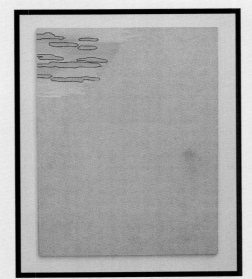

Backing piece, plain, painted with sky

The five layers, cut and temporarily assembled

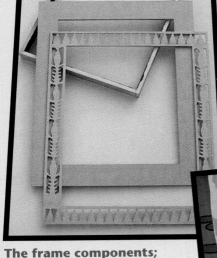

The frame components; box frame for layers, 6mm (¼in) MDF oblong frame, and fretted overlay

Close-up of Vasilissa and the white horseman

VASILISSA SHEET 1

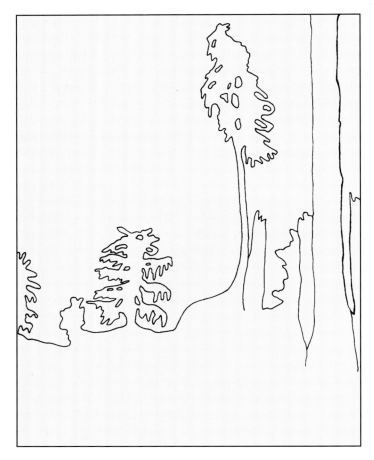

VASILISSA SHEET 2

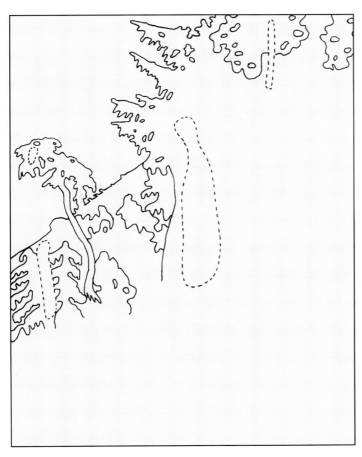

VASILISSA SHEET 4

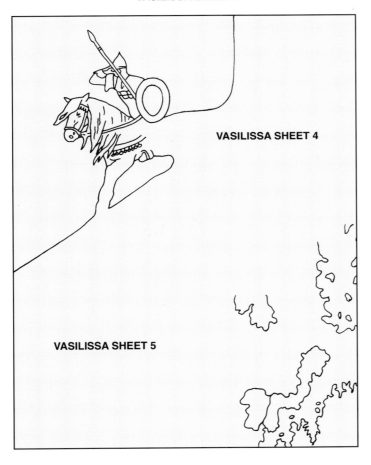

VASILISSA SHEET 4

VASILISSA SHEET 5

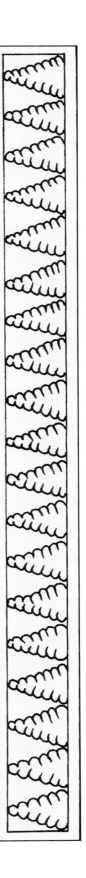
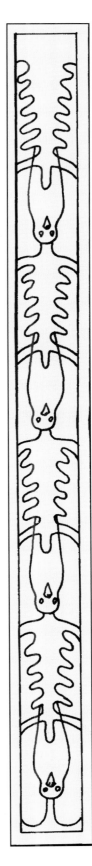

VASILISSA FRAME STRIPS

Riding with the Red Horseman

Terry Lawrence introduces the second of three horsemen interpretations

I
n the previous project chapter, I introduced you to Vasilissa and the White Horseman, an illustration by Ivan Bilibin to the 1900 version of Pushkin's fairy story *Vasilissa the Beautiful*. Now it's the turn of the Red Horseman.

As materials and construction methods are similar to those of the The White Horseman, I will give brief notes only here; please refer to the first article where necessary. The patterns for the various layers of the Red Horseman can be found at the centre of this magazine.

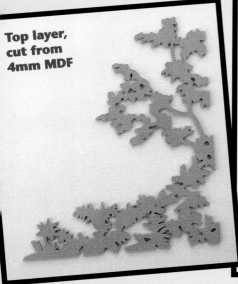

Top layer, cut from 4mm MDF

Top layer, painted

avoid breakage if you leave in place the internal cut areas whilst working. When you have drilled and cut each area, just hold the waste in position for the time being, using masking tape (top and bottom). You can remove this when cutting is complete and before you gently sand the piece smooth.

4 Assemble the sheets in order and you will clearly see where the backing sheet (No 5) of plain uncut MDF will need to be painted (i.e. between the trees of layer No 4 and above the horizontal of layer No 2) Mark with a pencil the limits of the painting on layers No 4 and No 5.

1 Cut four oblongs of 4mm (5/32in) MDF, each 340mm x 220mm (13 3/8in x 8 3/4in). For this picture there is also a fifth (top) layer, but it consists only of an 'L' shaped pattern of foliage, which is glued to the top sheet at the assembly stage.

2 Now enlarge by photocopier the magazine drawings to the size of the MDF sheets. For the first sheet (No 2) transfer the cutting lines of the drawing to the MDF sheet, using carbon paper.

By referring to the photos of the cut and painted layers, you will clearly see which lines represent the cutting lines and which are internal (painting) lines.

Cut the outline on the scrollsaw, using a fine blade (No 0 or No 1) and then sand the top and bottom faces of the MDF, before transferring the painting lines to it, again with carbon paper.

3 Do the same with sheets No 3 (the horseman) and No 4 (background trees). Then transfer the pattern of layer No 1 ('L'-shaped foliage)

to a sheet of 4mm (5/32in)MDF, 180mm x 210mm (7in x 8 3/8in) or larger. As you see, this is the most intricate of the layers of the picture and will become quite fragile as the cutting progresses. It will help you to

Materials

- 1 sheet 4mm (5/32in)MDF 915mm x 610mm (3ft x 2ft)
- 1 piece 6mm (1/4in) MDF 460mm x 314mm (18in x 12 3/8in)
- Craft acrylic paints
- Carbon paper for tracing
- Fine drawing pen (Edding Profilpen 0.1mm)

Second layer, cut and painted

5 Transfer the internal (painting) lines to the cut MDF panels, using carbon paper as before and paint with acrylics, using my colour photos as a guide. As in the case of the previous picture "Vasilissa and the White Horseman", you don't need to paint the cut edges of the layers; just the top flat surfaces. This is best done with brush strokes toward the edges, but if you do go over, you can scrape

The Red Horseman (third layer) cut...

...and painted

excess off with a scalpel when the paint has dried.

The photo process has modified the true colours a little, I'm afraid. The horse is actually a shade called 'Bonfire Orange' and is close to vermillion, whilst the horseman's boots and the horse's leather tack are scarlet.

Apart from the rider's sword, which changes from steel to a flame, no colour shading is required; just plain flat colours between the lines.

6 The frame differs a little from the first in the set, in that the picture is not central. The frame overlaps the picture layers by 3mm (⅛in) all round and the widths of the frame differ: the top of the frame is 55mm

(2⅛in) wide, bottom 70mm (2¾in) wide and the two sides are 50mm wide each, all around an aperture of 214mm x 334mm (8½in x 13⅛in). Cut this frame element from 6mm (¼in) MDF. In this case, I have rounded the internal corners to an 8mm (⁵⁄₁₆in) radius, but this, of course, is optional. The external dimensions of this piece are 314mm x 460mm (12⅜in x 18in).

7 The fretted overlays, as you can see, do not extend all round, but comprise two U-shaped frets. The top fret is cut from 4mm MDF, 314mm x 210mm (12⅜in x 8⅜in) in size. Its horizontal is 50mm (2in) wide and the sides 45mm (1¾in) wide. The bottom fret is cut,

again from 4mm (⁵⁄₃₂in) MDF, 314mm x 120mm (12⅜in x 4¾in). Its horizontal is 65mm (2½in) wide and the sides again 45mm (1¾in) wide.

Cut these two frets, then sand and glue to the frame. When dry, you can paint, stain or both. I first stained the frame (omitting the back face, but including all the cut edges) with Colron Pitch Pine wood stain and allowed it to dry overnight. Next day, I painted the surfaces of the fretted flowers and leaves.

Back panel (uncut) painted

Fourth layer, cut...

...and painted

8 Make up a simple box of softwood strip 20mm x 10mm (¾in x ⅜in), with its internal dimensions matching the size of the picture layers – 340mm x 220mm (13⅜in x 8¾in). Pin and glue, checking the corners with a square. Stain the inside face (I used Chestnut green stain). Glue this box to the back of the frame, ensuring that the MDF overlaps the inside measurements of the softwood box 3mm (⅛in) all round.

9 Fix the layers of the picture (No 2–No 5) inside the box, securing with tacks or MDF straps (see photo). These layers do not need to be glued together; they are best left separate.

10 Finally, place the foliage overlay (No 1) in position at the bottom right-hand corner of the picture, sanding its edges if necessary to butt to the internal edge of the frame (curve the corner if you have radiused the frame corners).

The five panels assembled

Top and bottom frets for frame, cut...

...and assembled

Scratch layer No 2 in a few places, under areas of layer No 1 foliage, using a scalpel and, with a few drops of Superglue (medium viscosity cyanoacrylate) glue the foliage into position. You are now ready to hang your picture. The final member of the trio, "The Black Horseman", follows in the next project chapter of this book.

Rear of frame, showing panels retained with MDF straps

THE RED HORSEMAN 1

THE RED HORSEMAN 2

THE RED HORSEMAN 3

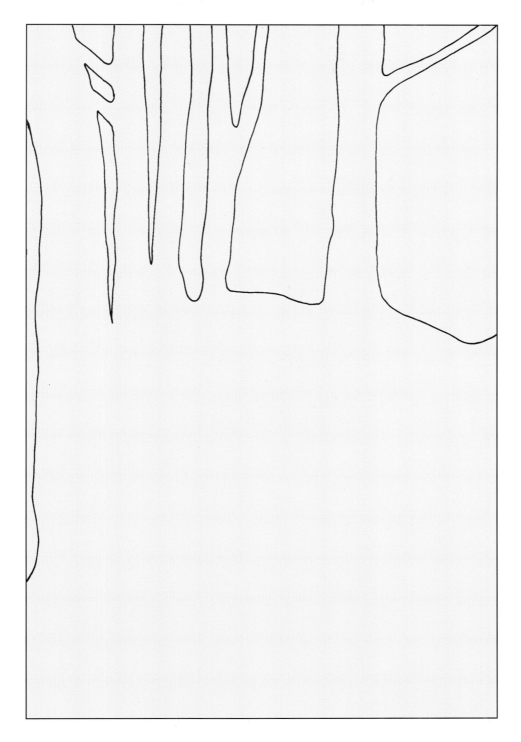

THE RED HORSEMAN 4

THE RED HORSEMAN 5

Black Horseman

Terry Lawrence presents the third and final multi-layered, three-dimensional picture in the set. All have been based on Ivan Bilibin's watercolour illustrations of 1900 for Pushkin's story "Vasilissa the Beautiful".

As in the case of the previous article – the Red Horseman – the materials and construction methods are similar to the first picture "Vasilissa and the White Horseman". So here I will give only a brief outline of the sequence, plus details of any variations. Please refer to the first article if necessary.

The drawings for the Black Horseman will be found in the Patterns section that follows.

1 Cut four oblongs of 4mm MDF, each 230mm x 310mm. Three of these will be cut on the scrollsaw and the last will be uncut, but painted with the sky. In addition, you will need two small pieces of 4mm MDF for the tree/fern clusters which will be appliqued to the lower left and right corners of the completed picture, after the frame has been made. These two pieces should be 90mm x130mm and 125mm x120mm or slightly larger.

2 Next, enlarge the patterns on the photocopier to match the size given above for the main panels. The top layer of the picture is panel No 1, which is the horseman and his mount.

Transfer the cutting lines of the full-sized drawing onto the MDF panel, using carbon paper and a ballpoint pen. The cutting

balance the trees on the right of panel No 2, but you may prefer to reverse them. Try them in their alternate positions before painting.

Painting

7 Use my photos as a guide as far as colours are concerned and note also the areas that don't need to be painted at all, because they will be hidden by the panel or panels above them. You don't need to paint the cut edges of the pieces, just the top flat surfaces.

8 After painting, you can use (or omit, if you prefer) the fine Profilpen to emphasise the lines between areas of different colours and to reproduce the original style, which was basically a line drawing, coloured afterward with areas of flat wash.

Most of the acrylic painting you need to do is best done with a fine brush. I use Cryla No 0 and No 1, with a No 5 for the larger areas of a single colour.

lines are basically the outline of the picture elements and, by referring to my photos of the cut pieces, you will clearly see which these are. It is best to omit, at this stage, the painting lines, as you will need to sand the cut panel before painting. Cut the outlines on your scrollsaw, using a fine blade (No 0 or No 1). You will find a slow speed very helpful, but if you have only a single-speed machine, don't use finger pressure to force the MDF onto the blade; just concentrate on turning the piece on the saw table to follow the lines.

3 Use a fine drill to start the pierced areas. I used a 0.75mm bit in my Proxxon mini-drill for all the small piercings. The smallest, i.e. among the

branches of the background conifers, are best done with a small spherical burr in the drill.

4 The horseman panel is straightforward, but the third panel is quite intricate, which is why I have left this picture until last. Sand the upper and lower faces of the cut panel and then with carbon paper, transfer the internal painting lines to the MDF, making sure that the pattern is aligned with the MDF outline (hold it in place with masking tape).

6 In the same way, cut, sand and transfer painting lines to panels No 2 and No 3 and also the two small foreground pieces. The larger of these two is designed to go on the bottom left corner, to

Materials

1 sheet 4mm (³⁄₁₆in) MDF 915mm x 610mm (3ft x 2ft)
1 piece 6mm (¼in) MDF 340mm x 420mm
Craft acrylic paints
Carbon paper for tracing
Fine drawing pen (Edding Profilpen 0.1mm)
(NB. this pen is for finishing the lines on the panels after painting, not for tracing the design)

MDF, with external dimensions of 340mm x 420mm. I used 4mm MDF here, but the thicker one would be better. The sides are 58mm wide each, the base 63mm and the top 53mm, so that the aperture overlaps the picture panels by 3mm all round. The actual cutout is 224mm x 304mm.

I have created a little square at each corner, partly for design reasons, but mainly to hide the little 8mm thick block of that is necessary to secure the plane of the rear panel.

9 The rear uncut panel is painted to represent the sky and the simplest method of doing this with acrylics is this: first mark in pencil the area to be covered and then paint this with pale yellow. I used a shade called 'custard', but mix white and yellow if you prefer.

the top edge of the yellow area, using a large, soft brush. Repeat just under this first line and then, with the same brush charged with clean water only, run across the junction of the two hues. This dilutes the blue, so it fades to nothing. Take up any excess water and lay the panel flat to dry.

Frame

10 Now mix a small quantity of ultramarine blue with just a touch of black and make this mix quite watery. With the panel held at an angle of about 45°, and the top edge resting on the table, lay a wash across what is now

11 Like the frame of the Red Horseman, this one does not have its aperture centrally placed. It is cut, in one piece, from a panel of 6mm

12 Having cut the frame, you will need to decorate it and I have designed a simple corner piece, the drawing for which is given with the panel patterns. Enlarge this pattern to 150mm x 142mm, transfer to 4mm MDF with carbon paper and ballpoint pen and cut four of these frets. Cut two rose and leaf motifs in the same way for the centre of each side.

13 Glue the corner frets into place, flush with the frame sides and glue the motifs centrally as shown. When the glue is dry (remove any dried excess with a scalpel) sand the edges if necessary and stain the whole frame, including all cut edges, but omitting the back face. I used Chestnut black stain, which dries very quickly to a charcoal grey on MDF. Paint the fretted pattern surfaces with tan acrylic and set aside for the moment.

14 Make up a simple box from four strips of softwood, 20mm x 10mm in cross section, so that they enclose an area to match

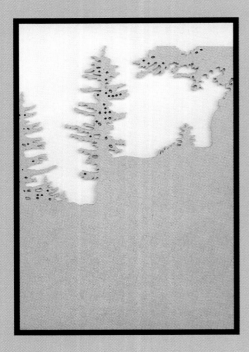

the picture panels (230mm x 310mm). Pin and glue these strips together, using a square to check the corners. I stained the inner face of this box black.

15 Now glue this box frame to the back of the main MDF frame piece, ensuring that the latter overlaps 3mm all round. You may prefer, for this particular picture, to secure the elements by gluing the panels, or at least panels No 1 and No 2, together, at the lowest part of their

faces where they are not painted.

16 Set the panels in the frame, then place the two foliage corner pieces in position (each with a square cutout at the corner, if you have made your frame like mine). Scratch panel No. 1 in a few places where these marks will be hidden by the foliage, and with a few drops of Superglue, fix them into position flush with the inner cut edges of the frame aperture.

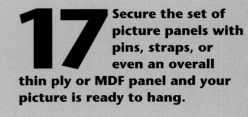

17 Secure the set of picture panels with pins, straps, or even an overall thin ply or MDF panel and your picture is ready to hang.

THE BLACK HORSEMAN 1

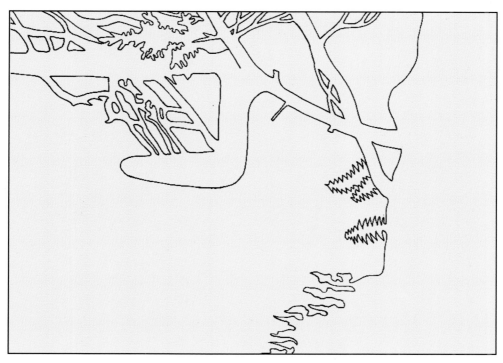

THE BLACK HORSEMAN 2

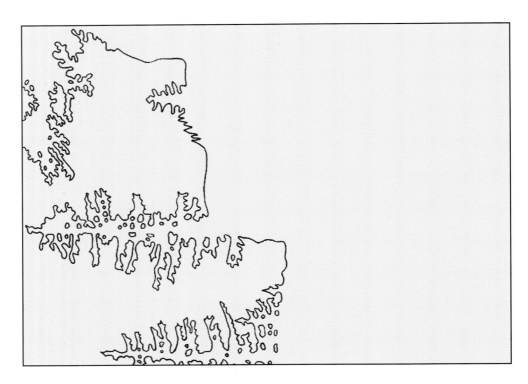

THE BLACK HORSEMAN 3

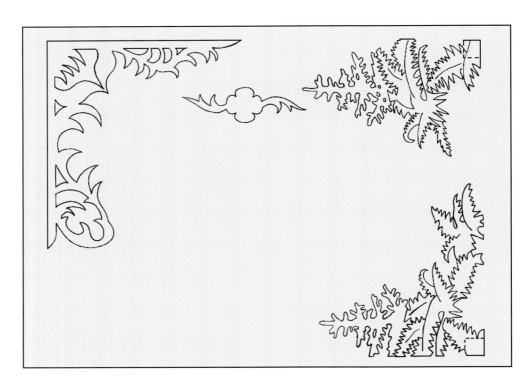

THE BLACK HORSEMAN 4

Jack Hudson puts the scrollsaw to work on this practical and easy-to-make set of table, chairs and bench for toddlers

Luxury dining

This simple and extremely useful set of nursery furniture is ideal for the family with one or two toddlers and their little friends. It will continue to serve their needs until they are at least eight or nine years old and it gives them their own private space away from the adult dining table. When not in use at feeding time it is the place for games, jigsaw puzzles, painting and rolling out modelling clay. All surfaces are easily wiped down.

Construction principles

Specially designed for the scrollsaw user and the home craft worker with a limited workshop, the assembly calls for careful and accurate working but no special tools. The square softwood legs are supported at the corners by the shaped panels.

It is assembled with 'screw-and-glue' and the following tips might help the inexperienced. Use modern metric Prodrive or Pozidriv plated thread- cutting screws. A power screwdriver is a great help, but not essential. Use 4 x 35mm (No 8 x 1¼in) screws for strength. The applied side and end panels need to have a hole to clear the screw so that it pulls up really firmly. When the two pieces are accurately located, use the screws as a punch to mark the legs and they will then cut their way in. Without the clearing hole in the applied piece it tends to climb up the screw and separate the parts whilst gluing up. The screws are sunk right in and the screw heads filled over with filler paste before final painting. There are special sets of drill bits that will drill the pilot hole, the shank hole and the countersink all in one operation. For unpainted wood use a plug-cutter set to hide the screw heads.

Materials

The side and end panels may be 9mm (⅜in) MDF or plywood. There is always some confusion about timber sizes because the USA has not adopted metrication. 9.5mm is nearest to ⅜in so that if you want to know the exact thickness of your material it pays to put several pieces together and measure them yourself. Similarly the table legs are sold as 50mm x 50mm planed softwood, which is near enough to 2in x 2in in imperial measure. In fact they come out at approximately 45mm x 45mm after being planed all round and the smaller square legs for the bench and chairs sold as 38mm x 38mm (1½in square) finish at 35mm x 35mm.

Use 16mm x 100mm (⅝in x 4in) tongued, grooved and v-jointed (tg&v) pine matchboard for the table top and the seats. You may prefer to use 16mm (⅝in) plywood or MDF for these flat surfaces, but the matchboard is inexpensive and gives an attractive knotty pine finish that will not warp in centrally heated rooms. It is better to put the v-jointing on the underside because chocolate, modelling clay and spilt milk might gather in the grooves when the furniture is in use. You may ask why buy v-jointed instead of plain tongued-and-grooved, and the answer is that until you get to the larger floorboard sizes it is not usually stocked at the merchant's. The 100mm (4in) width is reduced to about 87mm (3⅜in) effective width when the tongues are pulled into the grooves.

In the patterns, the most economical cutting-out layout is suggested for table, bench and chairs.

Materials List

Material	Quantity	Use	Approx. Cost
9mm plywood or MDF	4ft x 4ft sheet	Side and end panels	£8.00
50 x 50 p.a.r. softwood	About 3.3 metres	Table legs	£3.20
38 x 38 p.a.r. softwood	About 5 metres	Bench and chair legs	£4.40
16 x 100 p.t.g.v. matchboard	About 10 metres	Table tops and seats	£10.00
65 x 20 p.a.r. softwood	1 metre	Table cross batten	£0.40
Screws 3.5 x 30mm (No. 6 x 1in)	200 box	Plated cross-head	£1.45
Screws 4 x 35mm (No. 8 x 1 1/2in)	200 box	Plated cross-head	£2.40
Chrome furniture glides	16	Under the feet	£2.50
Finishing materials & glue		Paint, varnish, etc.	£4.00

Notes

• The above approximate figures are based upon buying in bulk from a merchant. The total cost is about £37 but you will have plenty of useful leftovers for future use.
• Timber merchants say "p.a.r" for planed all round and "ptg&v" for planed, tongued, grooved and v-jointed.

Suppliers

Axminster Power Tool Centre,
Chard Street, AXMINSTER, Devon, EX13 5DZ.
Tel: 01297–33656

Boddy's, BOROUGHBRIDGE,
North Yorkshire, YO5 9LJ.
Tel: 01423–322370

Craft Supplies Ltd., Miller's Dale, BUXTON,
Derbyshire, SK17 8SN.
Tel: 01298–871636

Hobbies (Dereham) Ltd.,
Dereham, Norfolk, NR19 2QZ.
Tel:01362–692985

W. Hobby Ltd., Knight's Hill Square,
LONDON SE27 0HH. Tel: 0208–7614244

Costs

It always pays to buy "in random lengths" from the builder's merchant. For example, do not ask them for "four 50mm x 50mm legs, 500mm long", but buy one 2m length of square stock and cut it up at home. Buy a sheet of 9mm MDF or plywood and ask them to deliver, and shop around the suppliers for smaller sheet sizes. As mentioned above, the USA and Canada dominate the world market and have not gone metric, so sheets are 8ft by 4ft, but many suppliers will do 4ft x 4ft or even 2ft x 4ft panels. The smaller sizes will go in the boot and a friendly storeman will usually cut long lengths of timber or matchboard to fit into your car.

Similarly do not buy screws from the superstores in expensive bags of ten but go for a box of 200. Keep to a few useful sizes and build up your stock over future projects.

Standardise! We must now accept Euro-sizes and cross-head drives, so go for a few boxes of plated thread-cutting Pozidriv screws. Start with 3.5 x 30mm and 4.0 x 35mm at about £2.00 a box.

The table, bench and two chairs cost me about £8 for 9mm MDF, £18 for timber, £7 for screws and glides, £4 for plastic coating and emulsion... say about £37 in all, including the glue. But I still have plenty of off-cuts for a future project or two. If you decide to use 9mm plywood, be prepared to pay almost twice the cost of MDF.

Finishes

All the MDF panels are painted with matt white plastic emulsion to give a firm sealed surface for the colour. Instead of the expense of buying different tins of coloured paint, why not buy some primary dyes and mix them yourself with the white emulsion to obtain whatever colour scheme you prefer?

The working tops are going to come in for a lot of punishment and in my opinion there is nothing better than Rustin's Clear Plastic Coating which is one of the toughest finishes available. It is a two-part cold cure finish. The hardener is mixed in a jar with the lacquer in the ratio 1:4 and will keep in the jar for several days in cool weather. It is brushed on and sets so quickly that four coats may be applied quite easily in a day.

I recommend four coats, with a light rub down between each, to build up a really strong protective surface that can be brought to a mirror finish with a cutting paste such as T-Cut or Rustin's burnishing paste. As the photographs show, the final result is very pleasing and it can be wiped down or scrubbed with hot water if need be.

Chromium-plated furniture domes are tapped into the underside of the feet for protection

The table
(See Patterns.)

1 The two long table side panels are cut from a piece 830mm x 285mm (32½in x 11¼in) and the two table end panels from a piece 560mm x 285mm (22in x 11¼in). Even more economically, all four can come out of one piece 1260mm x 330mm (49¾in x 13in).

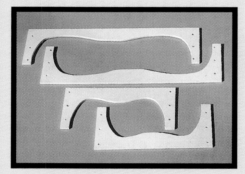

▲ Long side and short end panels cut from 9mm MDF

2 Draw the shapes of the panels on the MDF sheet. Set out the rectangles first. Mark down 200mm (8in) at the ends and 70mm (2¾in) at the centres.

Note: the long panels overlap the ends of the end panels so that the width at the leg is 55mm (2¼in) for the long side panels but only 45mm (1¾in) for the end panels.

3 Draw a nice curve for the first corner from the leg to the centre, trace it off and transfer it to a thin piece of card. Cut out this shape to make a useful template to get all the curves the same.

4 Because of the limitations of throat depth with a scrollsaw you may have to separate the pieces by roughing them out with a power jigsaw or a hand saw.

Note: a small hand-held power jigsaw may be purchased for under £50 and it makes a useful tool for a multitude of jobs especially cutting up MDF/plywood sheets.

5 Cut the square sides accurately and scroll out the shapes with a moderately coarse blade, say 2.8mm x 10 tpi.

6 Finish the sawn edges with sand paper, or a flap-wheel sander in the drill, and give them a coat of matt white emulsion.

7 Cut four 500mm legs out of 50mm x 50mm softwood.
Note: the more advanced worker with a lathe might like to turn the legs at this stage.

The four square legs and the panels ready for assembly ▼

8 Set out the screw holes carefully and drill with a 3.5mm bit and countersink. Set the screws 32mm in on the long sides and 22mm in on the short ends so that the screws are central in the legs and stagger them so that they do not foul each other.

▲ Table frame assembled ready for top to be fixed

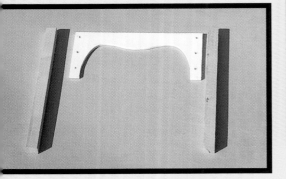

▲ End panel prepared for assembly

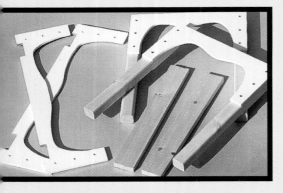

▲ End panels assembled with cross battens and side panels ready to fix

9 Assemble the two short ends. Position the legs carefully so that they are exactly square to the top. Use 4 x 35mm (No 8 x 1¼in) screws for strength and insert the six screws, without glue for the first fit-up.

10 Apply the two long side panels and insert the screws. These overlap the ends of the short panels. It is worth taking a piece of scrap wood and cutting it to the exact distance between the legs to use as a gauge to make sure that all the legs are parallel and true.

Tip: use a rectangular piece of MDF or blockboard with edge strips on two sides as an assembly table, like a small bench top and assembly will be accurate and easy.

11 Mark out the positions of the slots for the two cross battens 480mm x 65mm x 20mm (19in x 2 ½in x ¾in) on the long sides, just behind the legs.

12 When you are satisfied that the table is four-square unscrew it all.

13 Cut the notches for the table-top cross battens.

14 The finished appearance will be greatly enhanced if the corners of the legs are rounded over and sanded at this stage and you may chamfer round the bottoms if you wish. Finish them with Rustin's Plastic Coating before final assembly.

15 Reassemble the table with a good quality wood glue like the new aliphatic resin wood glues such as Titebond which are very good, or the two-part Aerolite 306 has amazing strength.

16 Fill the screw holes with a filling paste and sand off. Round all the corners so that there are no sharp edges anywhere.

17 Apply a second coat of white emulsion all round and the table is ready for the colour coats. After completing the colour scheme, varnish it over with the plastic coating to make it permanent and washable.

▲ Tongued and grooved pieces cut to length for table top

18
Make the table top from six pieces 775mm x 100mm x 16mm tg&v match board (30½in x 4in x ⅝in). Cut the tongue off one side and the groove off the other to give a finished width of 490mm (19¼in). Put a little glue in the grooves before clamping them up.

19
For a nicely curved end draw a radius of 745mm (29¼in) at each end and cut off. This is not essential but it improves the appearance. Round all edges and sharp corners. Sand off and brush on several coats of Plastic Coating. After two days hardening this surface may be burnished to a glass-like finish with a cutting or burnishing paste, if desired.

20
Drill and countersink screw holes in the two cross battens and pin and glue them in their slots. Turn the table frame upside down on the

▲ Table top glued together and ready to be screwed to cross battens

◄ The child's table, bench and chairs out in the garden and ready for use

Demonstrates the similarity between bench and table ▼

underside of the table, position it accurately and screw through the battens into the underside with 3.5 x 30mm screws. Put the grooved side of the top underneath to give a smooth top.

21
Put chrome dome furniture glides on the bottoms of the legs.

The bench

(See Patterns.) You may decide that you do not need a bench seat, but it is strongly recommended for the use of visiting playmates. The bench seat is simply a scaled-down version of the table and the steps described above are the same.

The legs need not be so sturdy and 38mm x 38 mm (1½in x 1½in) square softwood will suffice. The finished height of 300mm (11¾in) is just about right for any age from two to eight or even more. The larger 4 x 35mm wood screws give added strength but 3.5 x 30mm would probably be adequate.

The chairs

(See Patterns.) The chairs are like little thrones. They contain the smaller members of the family comfortably and are very stable. Toddlers will drag them around to gain access to things that have been put 'out of their reach'. This is unavoidable but it means that the bench and chairs must be sturdy and not easily tipped over.

1 Cut out the back rest and the front and back seat supports and drill and countersink them for the screws. Cut the sides from one piece 530mm x 345mm (21in x 13in). Drill and countersink them for the screws.

2 Finish all edges with sandpaper, or a flap-wheel sander in the drill and seal all round with matt white emulsion.

3 Cut the two rear legs 530mm (21in) and the two front legs 260mm (10¼in) from 38mm x 38mm softwood. This makes the seat height about 275mm (10¾in) – about right for the average toddler.

4 It is best to rebate the front and rear seat supports and the top back support into the legs. This is not essential, but neither is it difficult to do with a back saw and chisel, but a careful, worker will be able to do it with the scrollsaw.

5 Assemble the back and the front frames dry.

6 Fit the side panels and make sure that the finished chair is square and true.

7 Make the seat out of tg&v matchboard and cut out the square recesses for the rear legs. Round them so that there are no sharp edges or corners.

8 Apply the final colour coats of paint, varnish and assemble with screws and glue.

▲ Lobster cut-out on chair end

▲ Crab on chair end

▼ Seaside subjects on end panel

End thoughts

The set shown here was made for a family that lives on the coast. Accordingly blue and yellow (for sea and sand) was chosen as a simple colour scheme with seaside motifs, such as crabs, starfish and shells applied afterwards. Using acrylic paints (which dry hard and may be coated with plastic coating) the more artistic craft worker might like to paint pictures directly on to the surfaces. Cut-out

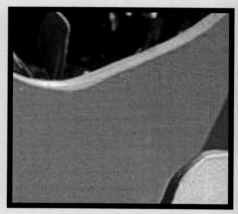

▲ Tropical fish on chair end

shapes, or appliqué motifs, are easy to cut on the scrollsaw in thin plywood and apply as low relief features.

Some may prefer a lot of bright contrasting primary colours on different faces using red, blue, yellow and green - the sort of thing that plastic toy manufacturers go for. A very experienced primary school teacher has told me that tiny children are not impressed by a mass of clashing colours and often show their budding good taste by preferring harmonious colour schemes.

Themes for the applied ornamentation might be chosen from nursery rhymes, flowers, cartoon characters or whatever takes your fancy. Whatever you do, have fun doing it and you will make a lot of little people very happy.

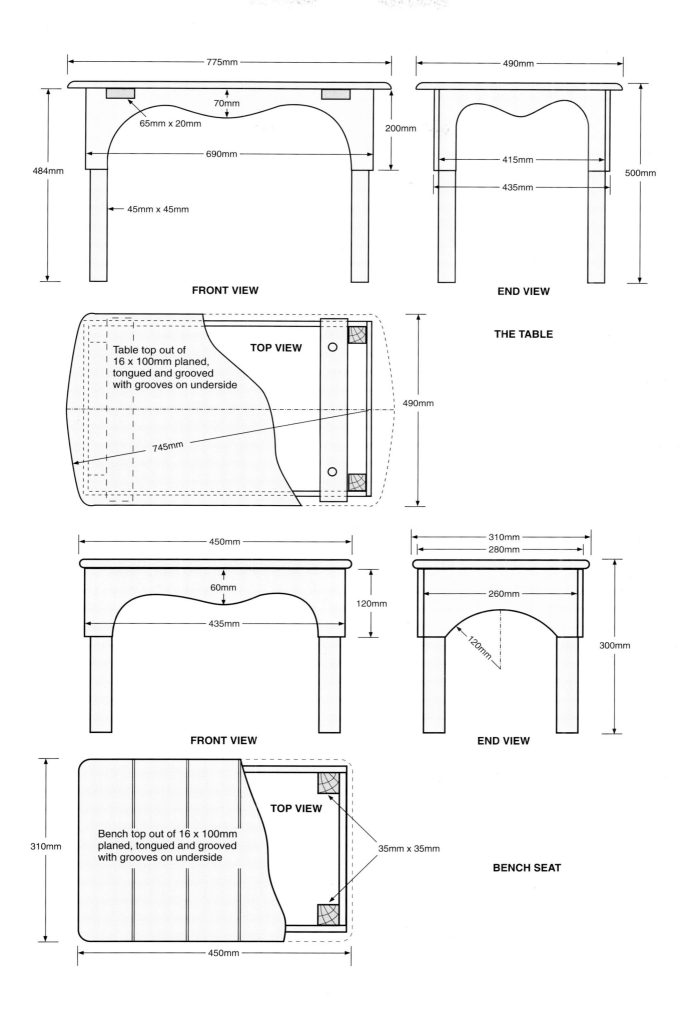

775mm

70mm

65mm x 20mm

690mm

484mm

200mm

45mm x 45mm

FRONT VIEW

490mm

415mm

435mm

500mm

END VIEW

THE TABLE

Table top out of
16 x 100mm planed,
tongued and grooved
with grooves on underside

TOP VIEW

490mm

745mm

450mm

60mm

435mm

120mm

FRONT VIEW

310mm

280mm

260mm

120mm

300mm

END VIEW

310mm

Bench top out of 16 x 100mm
planed, tongued and grooved
with grooves on underside

TOP VIEW

35mm x 35mm

BENCH SEAT

450mm

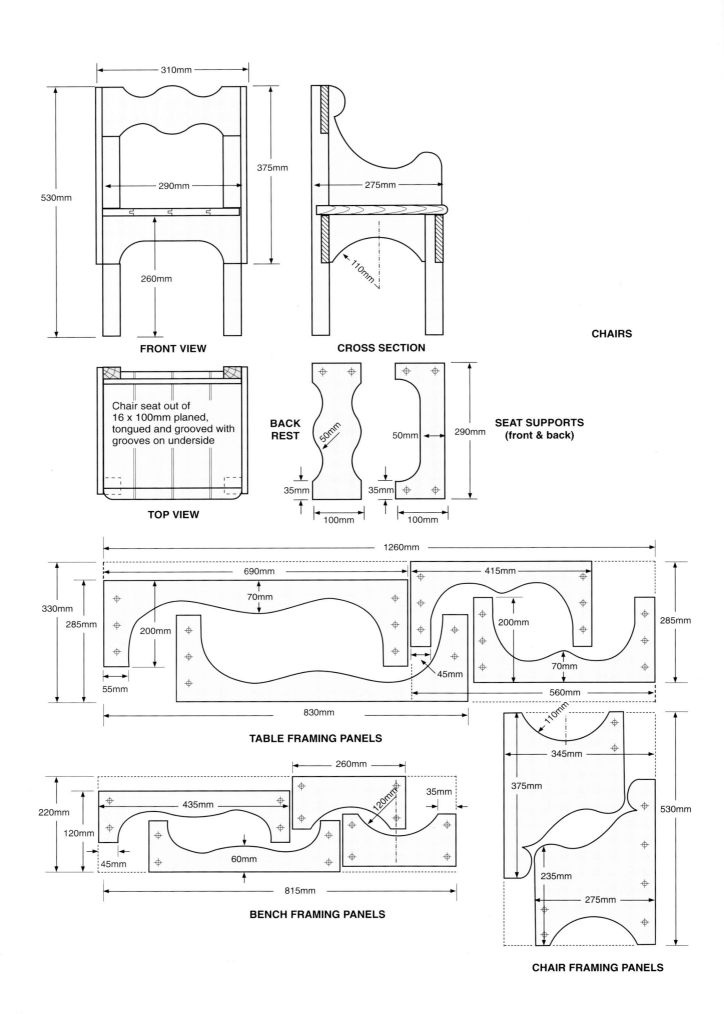

310mm

375mm

530mm

290mm

260mm

FRONT VIEW

275mm

110mm

CROSS SECTION

CHAIRS

Chair seat out of
16 x 100mm planed,
tongued and grooved with
grooves on underside

TOP VIEW

BACK REST

50mm

35mm

100mm

50mm

35mm

100mm

290mm

**SEAT SUPPORTS
(front & back)**

1260mm

690mm

70mm

330mm

285mm

200mm

55mm

45mm

830mm

415mm

200mm

70mm

285mm

560mm

TABLE FRAMING PANELS

260mm

220mm

435mm

120mm

120mm

35mm

45mm

60mm

815mm

BENCH FRAMING PANELS

110mm

345mm

375mm

530mm

235mm

275mm

CHAIR FRAMING PANELS

Hall of mirrors

Sweeping lines in the Art Nouveau style make this hall mirror and coat rack by **Christine Richardson** a perfect partner for the period home

Hallways and entrances are always difficult areas to furnish; we want corridors like them to look tidy and welcoming to guests but they are often dark and cluttered. This space-saving combination hall mirror and coat rack will help reflect available light and ensure coats are kept in check. The fretwork cow parsley design adds interest and is an authentic Art Nouveau decorative motif.

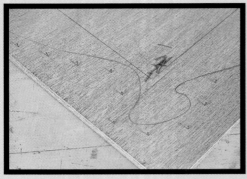

▲ Pin the three layers of plywood together with panel pins outside the cutting line

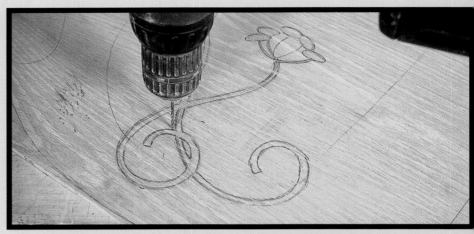

▲ Drilling holes for threading the scrollsaw blades for fretwork

Step by step

1 Enlarge the template provided. Stick the template to the front face of the oak-veneered ply with Spraymount. Although we have three pieces of plywood, we are only going to cut the outline once. To achieve this time-saving miracle, stack the plywood, starting from the bottom with the 9mm ply, then the 6mm ply and finally the veneered ply. From now on I will refer to these as the bottom, middle and top frame. Use panel

The three parts of the frame, showing the solid bottom frame, the middle frame with the opening for the mirror and the decorative opening in the top frame ▼

pins to pin all the layers together – outside the outline of the template in the waste area.

2 To cut any curved lines the coarser spiral blade is very effective, however it is impossible to keep it in a straight line, so for the bottom of the frame and possibly the sides you will need to change to the coarser of the two straight blades. Cut out the top of the frame first, including the little 'horns', then both sides and finally the base. As you cut away the waste and therefore the panel pins, the work will become more difficult to keep accurately stacked; if you have real problems, strap masking tape over the cut outline to keep all the edges accurately registered.

3 Now you have three pieces of plywood cut to the outline of the mirror. Take the top frame of veneered ply and use the small drill bit to pierce the fretwork. Drill a hole in every enclosed space of the design; between the flower heads and within the scrolls and the main mirror area. Clamp the smaller straight blade in the bottom clamp and thread through the

▲ All of the enclosed areas of design are drilled ready for cutting out

drilled hole in the main mirror area first, removing most of the area to the right of the flowers before changing to a spiral blade. Start with the smaller areas between the flower heads and in the scrolls without detaching the stems from the main frame. The flower stems are very slender when finished, so the idea is to leave them fully supported for as long as possible.

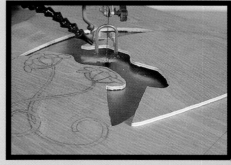

▲ First remove the large area of waste to the right of the flowers

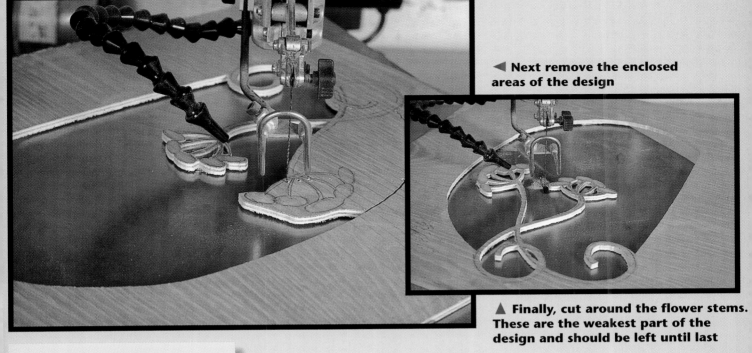

◄ Next remove the enclosed areas of the design

▲ Finally, cut around the flower stems. These are the weakest part of the design and should be left until last

Cutting list

- 520mm x 440mm x 6mm oak veneered ply (20¾ x 16¾ x ¼in)
- 520mm x 440mm x 6mm ply (20¾ x 16¾ x ¼in)
- 520mm x 440mm x 9mm ply (20¾ x 16¾ x ⅜in)
- 400mm x 240mm x 4mm mirror glass (16 x 9½ x ⁵⁄₃₂in)

Materials

- 4 coat hooks and screws
- 2 slotted mirror plates and screws
- PVA wood glue
- Spraymount
- 10mm (⅜in) panel pins
- 180g and 220g abrasive paper
- Small sheet of Funky Foam or similar thin foam
- Light oak wood stain
- Clear wax polish

Tools

- 22tpi and 40tpi spiral blades
- 22tpi and 10tpi blades
- 8mm (⁵⁄₁₆in) lip-and-spur drill bit
- 2mm (⁵⁄₆₄in) drill bit
- Flat wood rasp

4 Having removed all the waste from the mirror area, clamp your work in a vice and sand the inside edge, being sure not to place undue pressure on weak areas. Remove the paper template.

5 Stack the middle frame with the top frame above and use it as a template to draw the internal outline with the flowers onto the middle frame. Remove the top frame. Now cover the drawn outline on the middle frame with the mirror. Now draw around the mirror. This rectangular outline is the final piece to be cut out on the scrollsaw. Drill a hole for threading the straight blade as before, and cut out the space for the mirror, and check that the mirror fits. Once sandwiched between the top and bottom frames only the middle frame can be seen at the edge, not the mirror.

Drill out the area that will be behind the slot of the mirror plate, and drill pilot holes for its screws ▶

You will see from the pictures that the internal frame opening was too large for the mirror to sit completely within the external outline of the frame without removing the top left corner of the mirror. You can either do this yourself by scoring with a glass cutter and then snapping the piece off (wear gloves please!) or ask the glass suppliers to do this when they cut the mirror.

6 Position the bottom frame face down with the middle frame on top, using this as a template to draw the outline of the

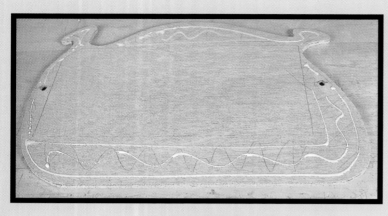

◀ Spread glue on the bottom frame, avoiding the mirror area in the centre

7 Turn the bottom frame face up, and apply wood glue up to the edge and the opening for the mirror in the middle frame. Position the middle frame on top, then panel pin these two frames together at equal intervals, about 10mm in from the edges. Position a layer of Funky Foam or other thin foam, no more than 2mm thick, in the centre of the opening for the mirror. Glue in position. The foam gives the mirror support and ensures that it will not move. Place the glass in the frame, apply glue as before and position the top frame. Check that the edges are registered all the way around and then clamp in at least six places – use scrap pieces of wood between the clamp and the work to prevent marking.

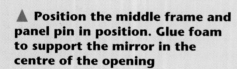
▲ Position the middle frame and panel pin in position. Glue foam to support the mirror in the centre of the opening

mirror. Remove the middle frame and position the mirror plates on the back of the bottom frame, one on each side and level with each other. Adjust them until the holes for the screws do not overlap the drawn outline of the mirror. The reason for this is to avoid the glass when screwing on the mirror plates. Mark the screw holes and the outline of the slots with a pencil. Support the bottom frame on some waste wood and use the lip-and-spur drill to make two holes, within the outline of the slots, all the way through the wood, one centred at the bottom and another at the top, then remove any waste in-between with the drill or the scrollsaw. Drill pilot holes for the screws with the 2mm drill.

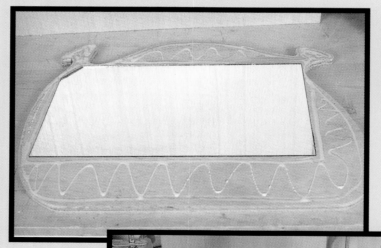

◀ Fit the mirror in the opening and spread glue on the middle frame

Position ▶ the top frame and clamp. Protect the veneer with battens of waste wood

8 When the glue is dry, remove the clamps and place the work in a vice then use the wood rasp to remove any unevenness in your cutting line, repositioning as you go. Finally, sand the edge of the frame starting with 180g and finishing with 220g.

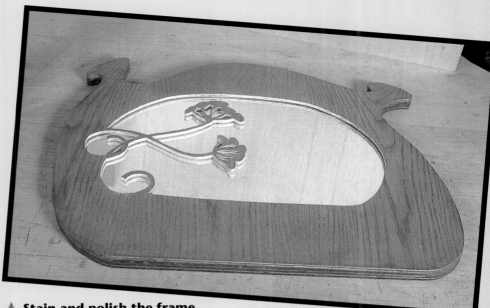

▲ Stain and polish the frame

9 Use a soft cloth to apply the wood stain with a circular rubbing motion. Try not to go over an area more than once as this will result in uneven colour. Also, try to avoid the glass – it may be possible to slide a piece of paper between the frame and the glass to prevent marking. When the stain is dry, wax with a clear wax furniture polish (not an aerosol) and buff to a dull shine.

10 Turn the work over and screw on the mirror plates. Turn to the front once more and position the coat hooks, marking the screw holes with a pencil. Drill small pilot holes and screw on the hooks. Clean the mirror with a soft cloth and remove dust from the intricate areas of the fretwork with a brush.

Tip

When remounting your blade always check that the teeth point downwards. Inserting the blade upside down will cause tearout of the wood fibres on the upperside of your work.

Screw on mirror plates and coat hooks for the finishing touch ▼

A moment of history

Terry Lawrence gives a brief history lesson with his interpretation of the Bayeux tapestry

An interpretation of three parts of the Bayeux tapestry, designed by Terry Lawrence

The Bayeux tapestry, which is actually an embroidery, is 70.1m long and 508mm high (230 ft and 20in), a little too large for the average person to reproduce. However, it seemed to me that a selection of passages from it, to a reduced scale, would make a fine scrollsaw project.

I have chosen three passages; the top details part of William's invasion fleet. The middle passage depicts the Norman knights riding out after landing at Pevensey. There is also a brief glimpse of Harold, instructing one of his scouts. The final passage gives a picture of the battle, with Norman horsemen attacking two groups of English foot soldiers. So, in three short passages, there is the variety of ships, horses and men, all at a quarter of the scale of the original.

All of the main pieces, individuals and groups, are cut on the scroll saw from 4mm (⁵⁄₃₂in) MDF. They are then painted and mounted on a baseboard. My base is again of 4mm (⁵⁄₃₂in) MDF, covered with bleached hessian, but you may prefer a wood or a veneered base. (See the photograph of the pieces on a plank of Contiboard.)

The latin text is painted on small pieces of 2mm (⁵⁄₆₄in) MDF.

"In three short passages, there is the variety of ships, horses and men"

Materials required

- **4mm (⁵⁄₃₂in) MDF**
  2 sheets 914mm x 610mm (3ft x 2 ft) will be ample (1 sheet for the figures, 1 sheet for the baseboard)
- **2mm (⁵⁄₁₆in) MDF**
  approx. 300 x 300mm (1 sq ft)
- **Cloth**
  0.5m (20in) of bleached hessian, 1m (3ft 3in) wide
- **Paints**
  Craft acrylics in eight shades

1 Each piece or group should be individually transferred to the 4mm MDF.

First enlarge the drawings by photocopier to the size required. My pieces average 90mm (3½in) high for the horsemen and foot soldiers and 95mm (3¾in) for the larger ships. William's ship at the top right is 165mm (6½in) long. You can, of course, change this scale to suit yourself.

The simplest method of transferring the shapes to the MDF is to glue them direct to the surface (Pritt adhesive is ideal). It is then a straightforward matter to cut around the outline. If you use this method, you will need an extra copy of the enlarged

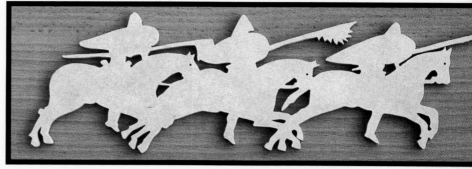

▲ A group of three horsemen, cut, drilled and sanded

the unwanted paper pattern and also cleaned the furry bottom edge, leaving each piece as though laser cut.

3 You can now add the inner lines. Using your second copy over the MDF, secured with masking tape and with carbon paper beneath it, trace the

painting lines. No great detail is required, but you need to show where a horse's head is to be when it overlaps the beast behind it. You need to indicate the position of the heads of the men and horses on the ships, and so on.

I have simplified the original tapestry cartoon a little by omitting all the thin spears, except for the three horsemen at the centre. I have omitted the shields which were originally placed between the ships and all the rigging. I have also omitted all the top and bottom borders which, although possible, proved to clutter the picture and detract from the pattern and storyline. The dividers are simply wavy lines between the three passages.

The elements of the top passage ▼

▲ MDF with tracing glued on and another with outline cut

drawings, in order to trace or transfer the inner lines later.

2 Cut out a piece. All my pieces were cut on a 14in throat, single-speed saw, with a No 1 blade (25tpi)
When you have cut out a piece, drill for the pierced sections (a 1mm (¹⁄₃₂in) dia. hole is ample for threading the blade) and cut them out. Sand the top and bottom faces. I used a belt sander, which removed

▲ The invasion fleet, painted

Painting

I used craft acrylic paints throughout, obtainable very cheaply from art shops in 2oz bottles. Different brands vary, but you can expect to find about 50 colours in a range, so you do not need to mix unless you wish. I used No 0 and No 1 Prolene art brushes.

The original tapestry was stitched with only eight colours, but some have faded a bit, despite being earth colours (for example, the black in the printed reproduction I have faded in parts to indigo). I have not followed the original faithfully, but have used a similar palette of (and please excuse the non-artistic names!) custard, yellow, caramel, terracotta, maple, burnt umber, avocado, bonfire orange, plus black and white. The paints are quick-drying, so wash your brush frequently. They are also strongly opaque, so don't worry if you go over a line; you can correct it easily with another application over the excess. Also, you only need to paint areas flat – there is no shading to worry about.

As long as you try to avoid say, two adjacent horses in the

▲ The middle passage elements

▲ The lower passage elements

4 I have provided photos of each of the three groups of pieces, both before and after painting. The former clearly show the piercings which you need to cut (though you can omit the smallest if you wish, as they do not show up well after the painting).

▼ The Norman horsemen, painted

It would have been very nice to have had a quick tensioning device when re-threading the blade for all these pierced areas, but even without, I could cut the outline of a large group in a fairly short time. It took me about 12 hours to cut out all the pieces for this picture and about the same for the painting. Incidentally, all the horses' eyes were drilled with a 0.5mm drill bit in a minidrill.

The battle: horsemen and foot soldiers, painted

The position of the words can be seen in the photo of the finished picture, but feel free to adjust them if you wish.

The texts are:
(A) Navigio: mare transivit et veniunt ad Pevenesae. (B) et venerunt ad prelium contra Haroldum rege. Hic Willelmi. nuntiat Haroldum rege de

and glue it to the board. I applied Unibond to the board, which was then placed glue side down over the cloth on a flat surface covered with a plastic sheet. When dry, you can trim the excess cloth with a scalpel.

9

With the pieces laid out on this baseboard, you can cut the two divider lines, approximately 762mm (30in) long, either straight or wavy, from 4mm (5/32in) MDF. I cut wavy lines as you see, about 6mm (¼in) wide. When marking the MDF, I laid the edge below the section to be underlined, so my curves did not overlap the bottoms of the ships, or the horses' hooves.

▲ The story elements, mounted on wood-faced board

same colour, there is no need to copy my interpretation or the original. This will be your picture, so do as you wish; the colour range gives the impression of the tapestry.

6 Text

The latin texts are all incomplete, of course, as I have taken passages out of sequence. In fact, in the bottom section, I have advanced and retarded some of the original text, in order to achieve a balance in the whole composition. As in the original, though, some words are split into separate syllables and I have retained the variations in the letter 'E' (uncial and roman).

7

Lettering, done with a No 0 brush, is about 10mm high and the individual pieces (with rounded ends) are cut from 2mm (5/16in) MDF which is first painted cream to match the base cloth.

exercitu. Willelmi ducis. (C) Viriliter et sapienter ad prelium: an glorum exercitu. Hic ceciderunt simul angli.

8 Base

Lay out the sequences on a sheet of 4mm (5/32in) MDF and check that you are satisfied with the spacings, between groups and between passages. Then mark to give a free border of about 50mm (2in) all round and cut an oblong to these lines – mine is 864mm x 457mm (34in x18in). Cut a piece of hessian (or another cloth of your choice) slightly oversize

10 Final Assembly

I tried out four glues before starting. Two were satisfactory; high viscosity cyanoacrylate (thick superglue) and Evostik Timebond. The former is rather expensive, so I used Evostik.

Having laid out all the pieces, I just lifted them one at a time, applied glue to the underside quite generously but not near the edges and placed it back in position. Any pieces which had curved after cutting were held down with weights. You do not need to apply any glue to the hessian; just to the MDF.

The panel is now ready to frame and hang.

◄ The completed picture, mounted on bleached hessian and framed

In this final section, **Jeff Loader** deals with the techniques required for advanced cutting operations

Advanced cutting

You may find that the blade aperture on the table of your machine is too large to cut small or delicate items comfortably and safely. While cutting, this could result in the blade trying to pull a small component down into the aperture, and there is then a risk that you cut your fingers.

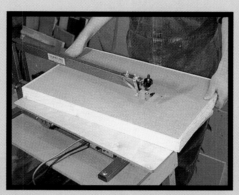

▲ **Large overlay table being fitted**

▲ **An overlay table temporarily secured with tape**

As a remedy, you can securely tape a temporary overlay onto the machine's table. This consists of a piece of 3mm (⅛in) material (such as ply or hardboard) with a small hole through it for the blade. The diameter of this hole needs to be marginally larger than the width of the blade. The size of the overlay required depends upon your preference and the size of your machine's table.

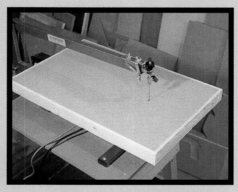

▲ **Large overlay table fitted to machine**

Large Overlay Table

With most scrollsaws, the stroke length (the vertical up/down movement of the blade) does not usually exceed 25mm (1in). This relatively short blade movement, especially when cutting thin materials, results in only a few of the blade's teeth being used. When these

become blunt, the blade is discarded with most of its teeth still sharp! To remedy this, a more substantial overlay table to the one previously described, can be made to fit over your machine's table when the blade's teeth become blunt from use. The overlay will increase the table's working height, thus utilising some of the blade's sharp, unused teeth.

I have constructed my overlay table from 18mm (¾in) MDF and have attached timber edging all round to prevent any movement during use.

To make a large overlay for a machine with an irregular shaped table you:

1 Place the MDF onto the table and mark around its shape.
2 Cut the shape out and drill the blade aperture hole.
3 Make and fit a few small 'lugs' (narrow strips of timber) strategically to the edge of the MDF shape. These lugs will hold the table in position during use.

Angled Cuts

Most scrollsaw tables can be tilted from 0° through to 45° (and often a few degrees more) thus allowing you to make a series of angled cuts. The tilting mechanisms on some machines are graded in degrees and accurate adjustment is usually straightforward.

For machines which do not have graduated degrees marked, or those that have one of dubious accuracy, a protractor will assist you to set the blade quickly to the required angle. If you use a shop-bought one ensure it is of the type that has

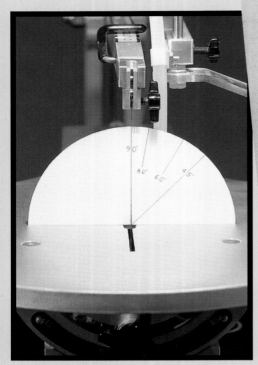

▲ A home made protractor will assist you to set the table/blade to the required angle

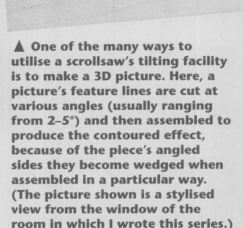

▲ One of the many ways to utilise a scrollsaw's tilting facility is to make a 3D picture. Here, a picture's feature lines are cut at various angles (usually ranging from 2–5°) and then assembled to produce the contoured effect, because of the piece's angled sides they become wedged when assembled in a particular way. (The picture shown is a stylised view from the window of the room in which I wrote this series.)

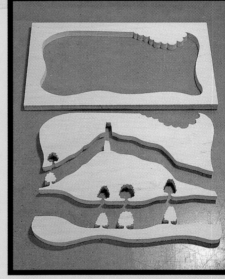

▲ The pieces of the picture cut out ready for assembly

Panel pins used to secure stacks of plywood prior to 'multi-cutting' animal shapes for Acorn Farm (see *Fun to make Wooden Toys & Games – GMC Publications*) ▼

its 0/180° line exactly on its base edge. Otherwise, you will set your table to the wrong angle. I use a simple homemade protractor constructed from card. I find that this suits my requirements more than adequately.

Multiple Cuts

Occasionally you may need to cut multiples of a shape in thin material. You can save time by stacking and temporarily securing several sheets together and cutting one thick shape from it. When the shape is unstacked you will have multiples of that shape. There are various methods of temporarily securing a stack including:

Edge taping – masking tape is stuck to the stack's edge. A drawback with this is that the stack's edges need to be even and square. Also the required shapes may be liable to movement during final cutting.

Double-sided tape – strips of double sided tape is applied between each sheet in the stack.

Pinning – moulding or panel pins are driven into the stack securing each sheet. Ensure that the pins do not protrude through the bottom sheet, as their points

will score the surface of your machine's table. If the shapes being cut are to be painted, you may drive pins through them (and fill the resulting holes with filler later). If they are not to be painted, drive the pins into the waste areas only. Ensure that the heads of the pins protrude from the top sheet to allow straightforward removal.

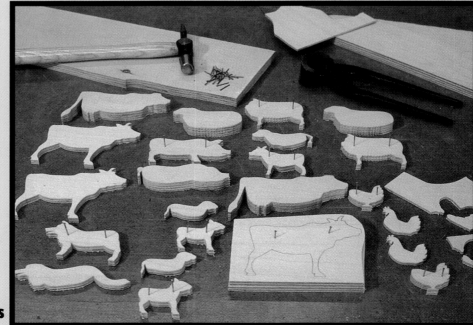

▲ Acorn Farm

▲ Compound
cutting – the profile and the
waste sections, after cutting

Cutting an
Acute Angle

It can prove difficult to turn the blade
when cutting along lines that form an
acute angle, especially when using a
relatively wide blade. The obvious
solution would be to reverse the blade out
and cut into the angle along the other line.
However, this is not always practical or
possible. A solution is to reverse the blade
out and then reverse it in again. You will
then be able to cut along the line with
little difficulty.

Compound
Cutting

Put simply, this is where a component is
cut in two planes to produce a three-
dimensional shape.

Furniture makers may be familiar with
this process when using a bandsaw to cut
out a cabriole leg. One side's curves are
cut and the waste is temporarily taped

back on, allowing the leg to be turned for
its other curves to be cut.

The patterns show the process for
cutting out a three-dimensional object, in
this instance a small polar bear. After
cutting the side profile, the waste is taped
back into position so that the plan view
can be applied. The waste also supports
the shape during cutting around the plan
profile.

When undertaking a cutting project
similar to the polar bear, it is vital that the
face surfaces of the stock (wood block)
are exactly square (at 90° planes) to each
other. Also you must ensure that the plan
profile is correctly positioned in relation
to the side profile.

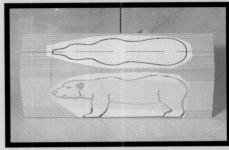

▲ Compund cutting – the waste
sections are taped back into
position so that the plan profile
can be cut

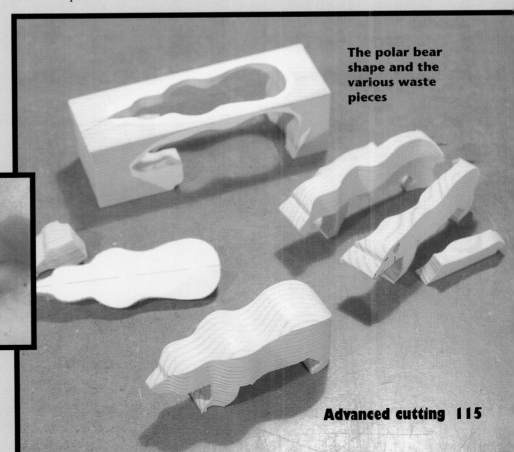

**The polar bear
shape and the
various waste
pieces**

▲ Compound cutting – the side
profile is cut first

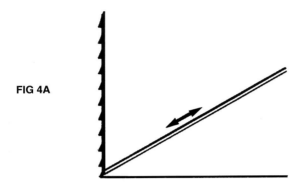

FIG 4A

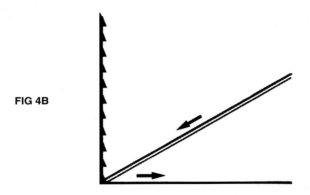

FIG 4B

Metric/Imperial Conversion Chart

mm	inch	mm	inch	mm	inch	mm	inch
1	0.03937	27	1.06299	80	3.14960	340	13.38582
2	0.07874	28	1.10236	90	3.54330	350	13.77952
3	0.11811	29	1.14173	100	3.93700		
4	0.15748	30	1.18110			360	14.17322
5	0.19685			110	4.33070	370	14.56692
		31	1.22047	120	4.72440	380	14.96063
6	0.23622	32	1.25984	130	5.11811	390	15.35433
7	0.27559	33	1.29921	140	5.51181	400	15.74803
8	0.31496	34	1.33858	150	5.90551		
9	0.35433	35	1.37795			410	16.14173
10	0.39370			160	6.29921	420	16.53543
		36	1.41732	170	6.69291	430	16.92913
11	0.43307	37	1.45669	180	7.08661	440	17.32283
12	0.47244	38	1.49606	190	7.48031	450	17.71653
13	0.51181	39	1.53543	200	7.87401		
14	0.55118	40	1.57480			460	18.11023
15	0.59055			210	8.26771	470	18.50393
		41	1.61417	220	8.66141	480	18.89763
16	0.62992	42	1.65354	230	9.05511	490	19.29133
17	0.66929	43	1.69291	240	9.44881	500	19.68504
18	0.70866	44	1.73228	250	9.84252		
19	0.74803	45	1.77165				
20	0.78740			260	10.23622		
		46	1.81102	270	10.62992		
21	0.82677	47	1.85039	280	11.02362		
22	0.86614	48	1.88976	290	11.41732		
23	0.90551	49	1.92913	300	11.81102		
24	0.94488	50	1.96850	310	12.20472		
25	0.98425	60	2.36220	320	12.59842		
26	1.02362	70	2.75590	330	12.99212		

1 mm = 0.03937 inch
1 cm = 0.3937 inch
1 m = 3.281 feet
1 inch = 25.4 mm
1 foot = 304.8 mm
1 yard = 914.4 mm

Imperial/Metric Conversion Chart

inch		mm	inch		mm	inch		mm
0	0	0	23/64	0.359375	9.1281	45/64	0.703125	17.8594
1/64	0.015625	0.3969				23/32	0.71875	18.2562
1/32	0.03125	0.7938	3/8	0.375	9.5250	47/64	0.734375	18.6531
3/64	0.046875	1.1906	25/64	0.390625	9.9219			
1/16	0.0625	1.5875	13/32	0.40625	10.3188	3/4	0.750	19.0500
			27/64	0.421875	10.7156			
5/64	0.078125	1.9844				49/64	0.765625	19.4469
3/32	0.09375	2.3812	7/16	0.4375	11.1125	25/32	0.78125	19.8438
7/64	0.109375	2.7781	29/64	0.453125	11.5094	51/64	0.796875	20.2406
			15/32	0.46875	11.9062	13/16	0.8125	20.6375
1/8	0.125	3.1750	31/64	0.484375	12.3031			
9/64	0.140625	3.5719				53/64	0.828125	21.0344
5/32	0.15625	3.9688	1/2	0.500	12.700	27/32	0.84375	21.4312
11/64	0.171875	4.3656	33/64	0.515625	13.0969	55/64	0.858375	21.8281
			17/32	0.53125	13.4938			
3/16	0.1875	4.7625	35/64	0.546875	13.8906	7/8	0.875	22.2250
13/64	0.203125	5.1594	9/16	0.5625	14.2875	57/64	0.890625	22.6219
7/32	0.21875	5.5562				29/32	0.90625	23.0188
15/64	0.234375	5.9531	37/64	0.578125	14.6844	59/64	0.921875	23.4156
1/4	0.250	6.3500	19/32	0.59375	15.0812			
			39/64	0.609375	15.4781	15/16	0.9375	23.8125
17/64	0.265625	6.7469				61/64	0.953125	24.2094
9/32	0.28125	7.1438	5/8	0.625	15.8750	31/32	0.96875	24.6062
19/64	0.296875	7.5406	41/64	0.640625	16.2719	63/64	0.984375	25.0031
5/16	0.3125	7.9375	21/32	0.65625	16.6688			
			43/64	0.671875	17.0656			
21/64	0.1328125	8.3344						
11/32	0.34375	8.7312	11/16	0.6875	17.4625			

1 inch = 1.000 = 25.40 mm

Index

A

acute angles, cutting 115
Altuglas 34, 35, 37
   friction-fusing 35, 36, 37
angled cuts 113–14
Axminster Power Tool Centre 90

B

barn owl wall plaque or clock 46–51
Bayeux tapestry panel 103–12
bench, children's 93, 95
Bilibin, Ivan, pictures inspired by 68–88
Black Horseman 83–8
blade apertures 113
blades
   remounting 101
   using unblunted teeth 113
Boddy's 90
bowl 3–8
bunnies project 13–18

C

calendar clock 62–7
candelabra 29–33
cast acrylic sheets *see* Altuglas
Celtic design jewellery 24–8
Celtic Knotwork Designs (Sheila Sturrock) 27
chairs, children's 94, 96
children's table and seats 89–96
clock calendar 62–7
clock movements 20, 47
clocks
   barn owl 46–51
   calendar 62–7
   mirror 19–23
coat rack and hall mirror 97–102
compound cutting 115
Craft Supplies Ltd. 90
cross, Celtic 26–7, 28
cutting techniques 32, 113–16

D

dining furniture, children's 89–96
dinosaur jigsaw 34–6, 38–41

E

Easter bunnies 13–18

F

finishes, non-toxic
   paints and varnishes 18
   vegetable oil 5
folding bowl 3–8
friction-fusing of Altuglas 35, 36, 37

G

gingerbread techniques 9–12

H

hair ornament 27–8
hall mirror and coat rack 97–102
Hindley's of Sheffield 37
Hobbies (magazine) 62
Hobbies (Dereham) Ltd. 47, 90
Hobby (W.) Ltd. 90

J

jewellery projects 24–8
jigsaw projects 34–45

K

knotwork design jewellery 24–8

M

mini-gingerbreads 9–12
mirror glass 20
mirrors
   clock 19–23
   hall mirror and coat rack 97–102
multiple cuts, techniques 114
   Altuglas 37

N

non-toxic finishes
    paints and varnishes 18
    vegetable oil 5
nursery dining furniture 89–96

O

overlay tables 113
owl wall plaque or clock 46–51

P

perspex 34, 37
pictures
    Bayeux Tapestry panel 103–12
    Black Horseman 83–8
    Red Horseman 74–82
    Vasilissa and the White Horseman 68–73
projects
    barn owl wall plaque or clock 46–51
    Bayeux Tapestry panel 103–12
    Bilibin-inspired pictures 68–88
    Black Horseman 83–8
    calendar clock 62–7
    candelabra 29–33
    Celtic design jewellery 24–8
    children's dining table set 89–96
    Easter Bunnies 13–18
    folding bowl 3–8
    hall mirror and coat rack 97–102
    jigsaws 34–45
    mini-gingerbreads 9–12
    mirror clock 19–23
    railway engine 53–61
    Red Horseman 74–82
    Vasilissa and the White Horseman 68–73
    Vasilissa the Beautiful-based pictures 68–88
protractors 113–14

R

rabbits *see* Easter Bunnies
railway engine 53–61
Red Horseman 74–82

S

safety
    blade aperture size 113
    hold-down on saw 32
sawing pressure 32
scarf woggle 24–6, 28
Scrollsaw Toy Projects (Ivor Carlyle) 53, 57
stack cutting techniques 114
    Altuglas 37
suppliers
    Axminster Power Tool Centre 90
    Boddy's 90
    Craft Supplies Ltd. 90
    Hindley's of Sheffield 37
    Hobbies (Dereham) Ltd. 47, 90
    Hobby (W.) Ltd. 90
    Yorkshire Clockbuilders 20

T

table and seats, children's 89–96
techniques, cutting 32, 113–16
three dimensional shapes, cutting 115
train, toy 53–61

V

Vasilissa and the White Horseman 68–73
Vasilissa the Beautiful (Pushkin), projects 68–88

W

wall plaque, barn owl design 46–51
whales jigsaw 36–7, 42–5

Y

Yorkshire clockbuilders 20

WOODCARVING

The Art of the Woodcarver	GMC Publications
Carving Architectural Detail in Wood: The Classical Tradition	
	Frederick Wilbur
Carving Birds & Beasts	GMC Publications
Carving Nature: Wildlife Studies in Wood	Frank Fox-Wilson
Carving Realistic Birds	David Tippey
Decorative Woodcarving	Jeremy Williams
Elements of Woodcarving	Chris Pye
Essential Tips for Woodcarvers	GMC Publications
Essential Woodcarving Techniques	Dick Onians
Further Useful Tips for Woodcarvers	GMC Publications
Lettercarving in Wood: A Practical Course	Chris Pye
Making & Using Working Drawings for Realistic Model Animals	
	Basil F. Fordham
Power Tools for Woodcarving	David Tippey
Practical Tips for Turners & Carvers	GMC Publications
Relief Carving in Wood: A Practical Introduction	Chris Pye
Understanding Woodcarving	GMC Publications
Understanding Woodcarving in the Round	GMC Publications
Useful Techniques for Woodcarvers	GMC Publications
Wildfowl Carving – Volume 1	Jim Pearce
Wildfowl Carving – Volume 2	Jim Pearce
Woodcarving: A Complete Course	Ron Butterfield
Woodcarving: A Foundation Course	Zoë Gertner
Woodcarving for Beginners	GMC Publications
Woodcarving Tools & Equipment Test Reports	GMC Publications
Woodcarving Tools, Materials & Equipment	Chris Pye

WOODTURNING

Adventures in Woodturning	David Springett
Bert Marsh: Woodturner	Bert Marsh
Bowl Turning Techniques Masterclass	Tony Boase
Colouring Techniques for Woodturners	Jan Sanders
Contemporary Turned Wood: New Perspectives in a Rich Tradition	
	Ray Leier, Jan Peters & Kevin Wallace
The Craftsman Woodturner	Peter Child
Decorative Techniques for Woodturners	Hilary Bowen
Fun at the Lathe	R.C. Bell
Further Useful Tips for Woodturners	GMC Publications
Illustrated Woodturning Techniques	John Hunnex
Intermediate Woodturning Projects	GMC Publications
Keith Rowley's Woodturning Projects	Keith Rowley
Practical Tips for Turners & Carvers	GMC Publications
Turning Green Wood	Michael O'Donnell
Turning Miniatures in Wood	John Sainsbury
Turning Pens and Pencils	Kip Christensen & Rex Burningham
Understanding Woodturning	Ann & Bob Phillips
Useful Techniques for Woodturners	GMC Publications
Useful Woodturning Projects	GMC Publications
Woodturning: Bowls, Platters, Hollow Forms, Vases, Vessels, Bottles, Flasks, Tankards, Plates	GMC Publications
Woodturning: A Foundation Course (New Edition)	Keith Rowley
Woodturning: A Fresh Approach	Robert Chapman
Woodturning: An Individual Approach	Dave Regester
Woodturning: A Source Book of Shapes	John Hunnex
Woodturning Jewellery	Hilary Bowen
Woodturning Masterclass	Tony Boase
Woodturning Techniques	GMC Publications
Woodturning Tools & Equipment Test Reports	GMC Publications
Woodturning Wizardry	David Springett

WOODWORKING

Bird Boxes and Feeders for the Garden	Dave Mackenzie
Complete Woodfinishing	Ian Hosker
David Charlesworth's Furniture-Making Techniques	
	David Charlesworth
Furniture & Cabinetmaking Projects	GMC Publications
Furniture-Making Projects for the Wood Craftsman	GMC Publications
Furniture-Making Techniques for the Wood Craftsman	GMC Publications
Furniture Projects	Rod Wales
Furniture Restoration (Practical Crafts)	Kevin Jan Bonner
Furniture Restoration and Repair for Beginners	Kevin Jan Bonner
Furniture Restoration Workshop	Kevin Jan Bonner
Green Woodwork	Mike Abbott
Kevin Ley's Furniture Projects	Kevin Ley
Making & Modifying Woodworking Tools	Jim Kingshott
Making Chairs and Tables	GMC Publications
Making Classic English Furniture	Paul Richardson
Making Little Boxes from Wood	John Bennett
Making Shaker Furniture	Barry Jackson
Making Woodwork Aids and Devices	Robert Wearing
Minidrill: Fifteen Projects	John Everett
Pine Furniture Projects for the Home	Dave Mackenzie
Practical Scrollsaw Patterns	John Everett
Router Magic: Jigs, Fixtures and Tricks to Unleash your Router's Full Potential	Bill Hylton
Routing for Beginners	Anthony Bailey
Scrollsaw Projects	GMC Publications
The Scrollsaw: Twenty Projects	John Everett
Sharpening: The Complete Guide	Jim Kingshott
Sharpening Pocket Reference Book	Jim Kingshott
Space-Saving Furniture Projects	Dave Mackenzie
Stickmaking: A Complete Course	Andrew Jones & Clive George
Stickmaking Handbook	Andrew Jones & Clive George
Test Reports: The Router and Furniture & Cabinetmaking	
	GMC Publications
Veneering: A Complete Course	Ian Hosker
Woodfinishing Handbook (Practical Crafts)	Ian Hosker
Woodworking with the Router: Professional Router Techniques any Woodworker can Use	
	Bill Hylton & Fred Matlack
The Workshop	Jim Kingshott

UPHOLSTERY

The Upholsterer's Pocket Reference Book	David James
Upholstery: A Complete Course (Revised Edition)	David James
Upholstery Restoration	David James
Upholstery Techniques & Projects	David James
Upholstery Tips and Hints	David James

TOYMAKING

Designing & Making Wooden Toys	Terry Kelly
Fun to Make Wooden Toys & Games	Jeff & Jennie Loader
Restoring Rocking Horses	Clive Green & Anthony Dew
Scrollsaw Toy Projects	Ivor Carlyle
Scrollsaw Toys for All Ages	Ivor Carlyle
Wooden Toy Projects	GMC Publications

DOLLS' HOUSES AND MINIATURES

Architecture for Dolls' Houses _Joyce Percival_
A Beginners' Guide to the Dolls' House Hobby _Jean Nisbett_
Celtic, Medieval and Tudor Wall Hangings in 1/12 Scale Needlepoint
Sandra Whitehead
The Complete Dolls' House Book _Jean Nisbett_
The Dolls' House 1/24 Scale: A Complete Introduction _Jean Nisbett_
Dolls' House Accessories, Fixtures and Fittings _Andrea Barham_
Dolls' House Bathrooms: Lots of Little Loos _Patricia King_
Dolls' House Fireplaces and Stoves _Patricia King_
Easy to Make Dolls' House Accessories _Andrea Barham_
Heraldic Miniature Knights _Peter Greenhill_
How to Make Your Dolls' House Special: Fresh Ideas for Decorating
Beryl Armstrong
Make Your Own Dolls' House Furniture _Maurice Harper_
Making Dolls' House Furniture _Patricia King_
Making Georgian Dolls' Houses _Derek Rowbottom_
Making Miniature Gardens _Freida Gray_
Making Miniature Oriental Rugs & Carpets _Meik & Ian McNaughton_
Making Period Dolls' House Accessories _Andrea Barham_
Making 1/12 Scale Character Figures _James Carrington_
Making Tudor Dolls' Houses _Derek Rowbottom_
Making Victorian Dolls' House Furniture _Patricia King_
Miniature Bobbin Lace _Roz Snowden_
Miniature Embroidery for the Georgian Dolls' House _Pamela Warner_
Miniature Embroidery for the Victorian Dolls' House _Pamela Warner_
Miniature Needlepoint Carpets _Janet Granger_
More Miniature Oriental Rugs & Carpets _Meik & Ian McNaughton_
Needlepoint 1/12 Scale: Design Collections for the Dolls' House
Felicity Price
The Secrets of the Dolls' House Makers _Jean Nisbett_

CRAFTS

American Patchwork Designs in Needlepoint _Melanie Tacon_
A Beginners' Guide to Rubber Stamping _Brenda Hunt_
Blackwork: A New Approach _Brenda Day_
Celtic Cross Stitch Designs _Carol Phillipson_
Celtic Knotwork Designs _Sheila Sturrock_
Celtic Knotwork Handbook _Sheila Sturrock_
Celtic Spirals and Other Designs _Sheila Sturrock_
Collage from Seeds, Leaves and Flowers _Joan Carver_
Complete Pyrography _Stephen Poole_
Contemporary Smocking _Dorothea Hall_
Creating Colour with Dylon _Dylon International_
Creative Doughcraft _Patricia Hughes_
Creative Embroidery Techniques Using Colour Through Gold
Daphne J. Ashby & Jackie Woolsey
The Creative Quilter: Techniques and Projects _Pauline Brown_
Decorative Beaded Purses _Enid Taylor_
Designing and Making Cards _Glennis Gilruth_
Glass Engraving Pattern Book _John Everett_
Glass Painting _Emma Sedman_
How to Arrange Flowers: A Japanese Approach to English Design
Taeko Marvelly
An Introduction to Crewel Embroidery _Mave Glenny_
Making and Using Working Drawings for Realistic Model Animals
Basil F. Fordham
Making Character Bears _Valerie Tyler_
Making Decorative Screens _Amanda Howes_
Making Fairies and Fantastical Creatures _Julie Sharp_
Making Greetings Cards for Beginners _Pat Sutherland_
Making Hand-Sewn Boxes: Techniques and Projects _Jackie Woolsey_
Making Knitwear Fit _Pat Ashforth & Steve Plummer_
Making Mini Cards, Gift Tags & Invitations _Glennis Gilruth_
Making Soft-Bodied Dough Characters _Patricia Hughes_
Natural Ideas for Christmas: Fantastic Decorations to Make
Josie Cameron-Ashcroft & Carol Cox
Needlepoint: A Foundation Course _Sandra Hardy_

Patchwork for Beginners _Pauline Brown_
Pyrography Designs _Norma Gregory_
Pyrography Handbook (Practical Crafts) _Stephen Poole_
Ribbons and Roses _Lee Lockheed_
Rose Windows for Quilters _Angela Besley_
Rubber Stamping with Other Crafts _Lynne Garner_
Sponge Painting _Ann Rooney_
Step-by-Step Pyrography Projects for the Solid Point Machine
Norma Gregory
Tassel Making for Beginners _Enid Taylor_
Tatting Collage _Lindsay Rogers_
Temari: A Traditional Japanese Embroidery Technique _Margaret Ludlow_
Theatre Models in Paper and Card _Robert Burgess_
Wool Embroidery and Design _Lee Lockheed_

VIDEOS

Drop-in and Pinstuffed Seats _David James_
Stuffover Upholstery _David James_
Elliptical Turning _David Springett_
Woodturning Wizardry _David Springett_
Turning Between Centres: The Basics _Dennis White_
Turning Bowls _Dennis White_
Boxes, Goblets and Screw Threads _Dennis White_
Novelties and Projects _Dennis White_
Classic Profiles _Dennis White_
Twists and Advanced Turning _Dennis White_
Sharpening the Professional Way _Jim Kingshott_
Sharpening Turning & Carving Tools _Jim Kingshott_
Bowl Turning _John Jordan_
Hollow Turning _John Jordan_
Woodturning: A Foundation Course _Keith Rowley_
Carving a Figure: The Female Form _Ray Gonzalez_
The Router: A Beginner's Guide _Alan Goodsell_
The Scroll Saw: A Beginner's Guide _John Burke_

MAGAZINES

WOODTURNING ◆ WOODCARVING
FURNITURE & CABINETMAKING
THE ROUTER ◆ WOODWORKING
THE DOLLS' HOUSE MAGAZINE
WATER GARDENING
EXOTIC GARDENING
GARDEN CALENDAR
OUTDOOR PHOTOGRAPHY
BUSINESSMATTERS

The above represents a full list of all titles currently published or scheduled to be published.

All are available direct from the Publishers or through bookshops, newsagents and specialist retailers.

To place an order, or to obtain a complete catalogue, contact:

**GMC Publications,
Castle Place, 166 High Street, Lewes, East
Sussex BN7 1XU, United Kingdom
Tel: 01273 488005 Fax: 01273 478606
E-mail: pubs@thegmcgroup.com**

Orders by credit card are accepted